THE INCAS

THE INCAS

By Franklin Pease García Yrigoyen

Translated by Simeon Tegel

FONDO
EDITORIAL

PONTIFICIA **UNIVERSIDAD CATÓLICA** DEL PERÚ

The Incas
Franklin Pease García Yrigoyen
© Mariana Mould de Pease, 2011

Translated by Simeon Tegel
Original title in Spanish: *Los Incas*
Published by Fondo Editorial de la Pontificia Universidad Católica del Perú,
2007, 2009, 2014, 2015

© Fondo Editorial de la Pontificia Universidad Católica del Perú, 2015
Av. Universitaria 1801, Lima 32 - Perú
Tel.: (51 1) 626-2650
Fax: (51 1) 626-2913
feditor@pucp.edu.pe
www.pucp.edu.pe/publicaciones

Design and composition:
Fondo Editorial de la Pontificia Universidad Católica del Perú
First English Edition: January 2011
First reprint English Edition: October 2015
Print run: 1000 copies

ISBN: 978-9972-42-949-1
Hecho el Depósito Legal en la Biblioteca Nacional del Perú N° 2015-13735
Registro de Proyecto Editorial: 31501361501021

Impreso en Tarea Asociación Gráfica Educativa
Pasaje María Auxiliadora 156, Lima 5, Perú

Contents

Introduction

Celebrated in the history of civilizations, the Andes were home to numerous societies from prehistory until the beginning of the 16th century when, during the period of the great European geographical expansion, the arrival of the Spaniards put an end to the *Tawantinsuyu*, known ever since as the Inca Empire. The region has thus formed part of the historical experience of humanity and, since the historians of the Indies of the 16th century, has been incorporated into historiography.

The Incas inhabited Andean space. Along the length of the region, between Colombia and Chile, the mountain range reaches peaks of 6,000 metres. The highest altitudes are found on the eastern side of the Andes, between Argentina and Chile, but in those zones where the various ranges spread apart, there grew the *paramos* in the north and the *puna* in the south, elevated plains which comprised a specific landscape of high altitude deserts. West of the Andes, there are tropical forests in Colombia, Ecuador and the north of Peru, and then, further south, from the Peruvian coast to central Chile stretches a varied coastal desert crossed by transversal valleys, many of which are dry for part of the year. East of the Andes is found the vast territory watered by the Amazon River and its tributaries. In this book, dedicated to the Incas of Cusco and their time, the theme of the Andes is not just a mere formality, given that the presence of the Andes drew specific lines in the demographic distribution of the region, as well as originating specific methods of adaptation by the populations to a natural environment, *sui generis,* in and with which they lived. When the Spaniards invaded the Andes in the 16th century, they found a region both terrible and filled with grandeur, and over time a stereotype was generated which identified it as inhospitable. Certainly, the chroniclers of the 16th century left testimony of the ferocity of the inter-Andean valleys; they also spoke of the bounty of its temples, but at the same time noted the difficult conditions created by the great heights.

In the 1930s, the German geographer Carl Troll had drawn attention insistently to the relationship between the *puna* and high Andean culture, emphasizing the crops and high altitude pasture animals. And the chroniclers of the 16th century (Pedro Cieza de Leon, for example) had stressed the fact that Inca paths, and Andean paths in general, usually traced the highest parts of the terrain whereas the Spaniards preferred the lowest routes crossing the valleys. This natural preference of the Europeans was the result of their difficulties in adapting to altitude, and it helped to generate an image of the Andes as an inhospitable and difficult land. Following in the footsteps of Troll, specialists highlighted the adaptation of the Andean population to the high zones (Carlos Monge studied this in Peru) as well as the way this benefited them. Thus, John V. Murra developed the theory that privileged the simultaneous utilization of the maximum number of steps of ecological levels by Andean societies.

Even in the 16th century, the aforementioned Cieza de León called attention to the geographic classifications which the Europeans of the time introduced and learnt in the Andes. The example that he used was *yunga,* a term that the Europeans popularized for the coast, which was also known as the *llanos.* Cieza confirmed that the term was valid when applied to any hot and humid zone on the coast, in the highlands or the Amazon rainforest. It therefore dealt with an ecologically defined boundary rather than a geographic space.

Over time, the Incas acquired a historical image, initiated by the chroniclers who converted into history the tales that, with real communication difficulties, they gathered. Generally, they related to myths and rituals through which the Andean population explained itself. At the same time, the chroniclers used the European historical and mythological tradition, translating it to the New Continent and the Andes. In this way, men from the Andes and the Americas were transformed into descendants of Noah; American geography was nourished from memories of Mediterranean classics and of mediaeval travelers to other worlds. Even the local gods were identified with biblical categories, whether from Hebrew or gentile religion.

Modern historiography did not exclude such arbitrary criteria as these. In the 19th century, early archaeologists were able to accept that the Incas, like the Mayas and Aztecs, had formed part of an ancient *lost race* (Ephraim George Squier, for example) and in the 20th century, an author such as Louis Boudin achieved fame by popularizing a *socialist* image of the Incas. Often, as in the 16th century, historians sought to explain the Incas with categories from European historiography. Just as Europe had achieved a world economy, it was establishing a world history, generalizing a historical explanation of all societies.

This book aims to be an introduction to the Incas, an ordering of existing information. By its nature, footnotes have been omitted, but there is a bibliography of the classic texts of the 16th and 17th centuries as well as a basic list of modern authors.

Chapter I
The Andes, its History and the Incas

Inca History

Many theories have been presented regarding the history of the Inca Empire since, in the 16th century, the Spanish chroniclers first wrote about the rulers that Pizarro and his band found in the Andes. Initially, the classical chroniclers posited that the Incas had been present the entire period before the Spanish invasion, believing they were responsible for part of the construction of the social organization which they found and even affirming that before the Incas, only villages or scarcely organized human groups had existed. From the perspective of 16th century Europe, the chroniclers debated the probable duration of the empire of Cusco, viewing it either as a historical continuity of long duration, as in the case of *The Royal Commentaries of the Incas* by Inca Garcilaso de la Vega (1609), or as a rapid and violent expansion of the Incas across the Andes, as suggested, for example, by Pedro Sarmiento de Gamboa in his *History of the Incas* (1572).

This discussion regarding the antiquity of the *Tawantinsuyu* was related to the justification that the Spaniards needed in order to explain their own conquest, which would be just if the rulers of the

Andean area had been usurpers or "illegitimate" holders of power. For this reason, in the discussion of the origin of the Incas and the extent of their conquests, the Spanish chronicles of the 16th century presented the notion of a long reign in which the rulers had "inherited" power, from father to son, along European lines, in a civilized Andean way, all of which "legitimized" their power. Against this theory, other proposals—such as that of Sarmiento de Gamboa—the Incas were illegitimate usurpers and violent domineers, who had subjugated the "natural lords" of the earth. In this context it is difficult to ascertain the truth and it is worthwhile indicating certain elements that allow us to understand what the chroniclers collected orally from the Andean people of that time.

The chroniclers gathered oral traditions of various types, mainly myths and ritual dramatizations, which were not ordered or processed according to the historical categories of 16th century Europe. In order to obtain the information that they needed regarding the legitimacy of the Inca government, the chroniclers examined the ancient sovereigns, their deeds and conquests. For this purpose, they not only transferred to Andean America the existing notions of "legitimacy" and "inheritance" from Europe but they also identified the *Inca* with the European king. They introduced into the Andes the European notion of "monarchy" which presumed *a single* ruler, which is today disputed when one realizes that the political organization of the Andes was primarily dualist.

The chroniclers interrogated a history and received myths and oral traditions. The first spoke of the origin of the world and, in more elaborate cases, of varying ages or states through which the world had passed. Appearing in these accounts were the gods who had participated in the ordering of the world as well as the founding heroes who had realized the sacred arrangements. In a mythical universe, an image of the past presented itself which was not historical and which did not correspond, in consequence, to the temporal, spatial and personal categories that history consecrates. The chroniclers ordered—reordered—this information in chronological form, tinged with the presence of the "kings", in other words, the *Inca*s who had governed the *Tawantinsuyu*, considered from the historical, European point of view of the chroniclers.

In this manner, a history of the Incas was constructed that has lasted until the current century, when the archaeological studies initiated in the Andes in the 19th century and developed in the 20th century, and the recent development of Andean anthropology, allowed us to understand the affirmations of the chroniclers from new points of view. Years ago attention was called to the anthropological quality of the chronicles, which also dealt with the Andes from the perspective of Renaissance history; at the same time it became increasingly difficult to consider the historical claims of its authors as deriving from Andean information. Today, the historical vision of the chroniclers may be more easily contested, even though for a long time many of their frameworks will continue to reign at the expense of others. For example, the chronology proposed by these authors will continue to be an important point of reference for the last *Inca*s, even though we now know that the same *Inca*s, presented as monarchical rulers, formed part of a dual power structure that is today being fully researched.

But the chroniclers offered invaluable documenting of the lives of the Andean people, which at times goes beyond the pure history of the *Tawantinsuyu*, and this can be appreciated in the information of ethnographical character, sometimes referenced marginally in the history of the Incas which they wrote with European readers in mind. Thanks to an enormous amount of information offered by official and private documentation from the Spaniards of the 16th century, and in accordance with the archaeology and anthropology of the

Andes of recent years, it is possible to complement and reorder the information of the chronicles regarding the Incas.

The information about the Incas which can be found in the chronicles and other colonial documents is not uniform. Since the earliest contact, it must have taken some time for the Spaniards just to acquire the linguistic instruments necessary to gather and process the information which the Andean people were able to offer; equally, it took just as long for the Andean people, in possession of tools reciprocally acquired as a result of the Spanish invasion, to write in Quechua or Spanish an equivalent version, or one at least in conditions to be processed by European readers. This resulted from the fact that the Spanish chroniclers—the chroniclers of the conquest—provided little information about the history of the Incas, even though in many cases they left data of unquestionable ethnographic value, even as they began the elaboration of historical and cultural stereotypes which have lasted for centuries.

It could not be avoided that, in the 16th century, the chronicles included mythical cycles in their diverse histories. Neither were the Andean chroniclers, already immersed in a process of acculturation, able to avoid the inevitable construction of a history, even though in the last of these the use of European historical categories is more obvious, and the permanence of those criteria which governed the oral transmission of information, the traditional method in the Andes, more visible. At the same time, as the process of colonization advanced, the chroniclers acquired new and more complete information. After the early years, in which the chronicles fundamentally focused on relating the deeds of the Spaniards—the epic of the conquest—they took more interest in the *Tawantinsuyu* of the Incas and they sought to offer more systematic information about the Andean past. This tendency grew specifically in the times of the Viceroy Francisco de Toledo (1569-1581), when there was a concrete effort to gather "official" information, produced both by the descendants of the Incas in Cusco as well as through studies among the population. But none of this changed the situation of the chroniclers as collectors of oral traditions, and the chronicles continued as receptacles of combinations of myths and ritual dramatizations, transformed into history. In turn, the chroniclers were using the writings of their predecessors, utilizing topics established since the first authors wrote about the Andes, assuming stereotypes and maintaining the prejudices of their times. Specialists have allowed us to see that the chroniclers constantly copied each other and redrafted similar information, rapidly standardizing the oral versions which circulated at the time. Reprocessing that information is one of the fundamental tasks of contemporary Andean historiography.

The chroniclers were conscious of transcribing myths—the so-called "fables" or "legends"—regarding the allusive tales of the origin of the world or the beginnings of Inca domination in the Andean area. This occurred, perhaps, because they could not guarantee to their own eyes, or those of their readers, the verisimilitude of the information they were reproducing. However, they equivocated less in transforming into chronologically-ordered histories those tales which appeared linked to the personal biographies of the *Incas*. Today, when we look with fresh eyes at their descriptions of the deeds of the *Incas*, we can still see in these very chronicles the indubitable legacy of the oral tradition. There, we can appreciate, for example, the form, like a collection of myths, in which they spoke about a war which would have taken place between the Incas of Cusco and the Chancas—inhabitants of the zone around the Pampas River, north of Cusco—transformed into a story of the epic of the victor, who the chroniclers linked to the beginning of the expansion of Cusco across the Andes. The cycle of the Chanca war, already assimilated in the times of the *Inca* Pachacuti, was also associated in the chronicles

17

with a series of modifications in the organization of Cusco, generally linked to the organization of the state. At the same time, as the versions which were available to the chroniclers were closer to the times of the Spaniards and could be completed or reorganized with other information, it was easier from then on for the chroniclers to offer a better picture of the history of the successors to Pachacuti, up until the war between Huascar and Atahualpa, coinciding with the arrival of the Spaniards in the Andes.

The versions the chroniclers received from their Andean informants included dramatic representations, or the tales corresponding to them. The chroniclers themselves gave testimony to their existence, attributing to them the formation of an official history, although they also identified them as a type of Andean theater. There is some additional data that allow us to get closer to these dramatizations and their meaning, as many of them continued during the Spanish colonial period and even into the present, changed no doubt by time and due to the cultural modifications introduced into and experienced in the Andes since the 18th century. A good example of the colonial functioning of these dramatizations is found in the pages of the *History of Potosí*, written in the 16th century by Bartolomé Arzáns de Orsúa y Vela, who compiled information written by previous Spanish inhabitants of that city in the 16th century. Arzáns relates the festivals which were celebrated at the end of one of the civil wars between the Spaniards of the 16th century, in which both the Hispanic and the Andean populations of the city of Potosí participated:

> After fifteen days passed in which the inhabitants of Potosí solely dedicated themselves to attending to the divine services accompanying the Holiest Sacrament which, when uncovered, was declared by its patron, to the Holiest Virgin and the Apostle Santiago, they attempted to continue the festivities with demonstrations of various rejoicings. And putting this into effect, they began with eight comedies: The first

four represented with general applause the noble Indians. The first was the origin of the Inca monarchs of Peru, in which was vividly represented the style and manner in which the gentry and wise people of Cusco introduced the very fortunate Manco Capac I to the royal throne, how he was received as Inca (which is the same as a great and powerful monarch), the 10 provinces which he subjected to his dominion with arms and the great celebration which he dedicated to the Sun in thanks for his victories. The second was the triumphs of Huayna Capac, 11th Inca of Peru, which he achieved with the three nations: Changas, highland Chunchus and the Lord of the Collas, who was struck on the temple by a stone hurled by the powerful arm of this monarch and the violence of a catapult, stripping his crown, kingdom and life; a battle which saw powers confronted in the fields of Hatuncolla, with the Inca Huayna Capac upon a litter of fine gold, from where he aimed the shot. The third, the tragedies of Cusi Huáscar, 12th Inca of Peru,was shown in the festivals marking his coronation, the great chain of gold which at the time had just been fashioned and for whom the monarch took his name, because Cusi Huáscar is the same in Spanish as cord; the rising of Atahuallpa, his brother albeit a bastard; the memorable battle which these two brothers launched in Quipaypán, in which from both sides 150,000 men died; they subjected Cusi Huáscar to prison and undignified treatments; the tyrannies which the usurper committed in Cusco, taking the lives of 43 brothers who he had there, and the painful death to which they subjected Cusi Huáscar in prison. The fourth was the ruin of the Inca Empire; representing the arrival of the Spaniards in Peru; the unjust confinement that they subjected on Atahuallpa, the 13th Inca of this monarchy; the omens and signs which were seen in the sky and the air before they took his life; the tyrannies and pain that the Spaniards inflicted on the Indians; the structure of gold and silver that he offered so they would not take his life, and the death that they brought to him in Cajamarca. These comedies [to which Capitan Pedro Méndez y Bartolomé de Dueñas gave them permission to perform] were very special and famous, not just because of the cost of their scenery, the propriety of their costumes and the novelty of their plots, but also because of the elegance of the mixed verse of the Spanish language with the Indian.

The description adds that at another moment the festivities resembled Andean "processions", where people, agricultural products and animals from diverse parts could be seen. After this all the *Incas* could be seen again, seated on litters and with their traditional attire and attributes. In the list of the latter "… who was most visible … was the magnificent Atahuallpa (who until these times [the 18th century] is still held by many of the Indians as he is shown when they see his portraits) …"

The version which Arzáns de Orsúa y Vela offers has direct reminiscences from *The Royal Commentaries of the Incas* by Inca Garcilaso de la Vega, inserted intact because of their significance as they explain how, in accordance with the classical chroniclers, the Andean population was accustomed to transmit information about the past through representations of this nature. The classic chronicles mentioned that the same ceremonies were held in the solemn festivals of the *Tawantinsuyu*, including when a new *Inca* took power, when an "official version" of the deeds of his predecessor would be shown.

It is worth adding that there are many testimonies about this type of representation by the Andean population throughout the colony and even in the present. The authors of the colonial annals and of the accounts of these festivities have made us aware that similar dramatizations used to take place when a new king took the Spanish throne, for example, and also for other special solemnities. There is also evidence that during the 17th and 18th centuries some of these representations were staged immediately prior to Andean uprisings and for that reason the local colonial authorities recommended their suppression. Finally, colonial texts which reproduce these representations have been found—they are, in truth, the Spanish "scripts"—such as in the famous case of the *Tragedy of the End of Atahuallpa*, whose colonial Quechua text has been rescued in its totality.

A distinct, interesting question is the testimony offered by Arzáns regarding the prestige attached to the figure of Atahualpa in the 18th century, which tended to stand out in the "processions" of Potosí. This may be related to the earlier claim that the accusation of "bastard", which the Spanish chroniclers laid at him and which Arzans insisted on, lacked significance for the Andean population.

In this way, the mythical information, probably itself reprocessed in the representations mentioned here, contributed to a version that appeared to exemplify the past—presenting it as paradigmatic— and which certainly complemented the classic chronicles. It is very probable that much of the historical information which the chronicles present responds to the corresponding tales of these dramatizations, as appeared to have happened with those referring to the Inca conquests. Taking these as a model, it can be appreciated that the Incas began their conquests from the north, always leaving from and returning to Cusco, and continuing afterwards in a clockwise direction. Even considering that there are variants in the texts of the different chronicles, this information lets us explain a ritual representation of the same conquests. It also appears that these conquests, presented in a ritual context, formed a widening spiral, in such a way that each time the Incas went out to carry out conquests, it appeared that they were conquering peoples and lands that their predecessors had already conquered. Each *Inca* could thus summarize the history of the formation of the *Tawantinsuyu*.

Based on these claims in the chronicles, and leaving the problems of the debatable chronology to one side as an abstraction not always open to greater precision through archaeological techniques given the short period that the *Tawantinsuyu* lasted, we can today propose a new picture of Inca history, one that understands the chronology and succession of the *Incas* themselves as provisional, bearing in mind that the only information available on that subject is the contentious succession of wars and conquests. It is natural that the chroniclers organized the chronology of the history of the *Incas* using their biographies as a base, given that this was the norm in European historiography of the 16th century. It is also worth adding that any history of the *Incas* written today is able to draw on much information other than the chronicles, provided by the copious administrative documentation produced during the colonial era, and which does not suffer from the Cusco-centric character of the classic chronicles. These, shaped by the European experience of their authors, presume that information from the court in Cusco was more correct, and, in fact, the history of the Andean area was modeled from Cusco.

The colonial information to which I refer is constituted by administrative documents from visits, accounts, surveys of the population and the lands they occupied, what they produced and the way they organized their economy, censuses and even judicial and notarial documents from the Colony; in all these documents there is information about the inhabitants of the Andean area, often explaining their relationship with the Incas of Cusco in ways which do not always correspond with the versions of the classic chronicles. Collating all this kind of information into a whole that is broader than that from the chronicles, it is possible to provide a version of cultural, economic, social and religious history of the *Tawantinsuyu* as well as an approximation of its political organization. It is worth repeating that it is not possible to isolate Inca history from an Andean history covering a much longer period given that, as already stated, the Incas constituted the final point of a long trajectory of thousands of years interrupted by the Spanish invasion of the Andean area in the first quarter of the 16th century, a history that continued after this event in the life of the population which survived the collapse following the invasion and resisted the colonization in a long process of acculturation continuing into our own times.

The Predecessors of the Incas in the Andes

Before the Incas there was a long and complex succession of Andean organizations which, over a long period, today measured at around 10,000 years, gave shape to an organically structured society, with visible developments in economic terms, a rich network of roads and a complexity of social relations that easily aroused the admiration of the Europeans who arrived in the Andes in the 16th century. Nevertheless, initially it was difficult for the Spaniards to distinguish between the Incas and their predecessors, not just because of the fact, as previously stated, that the duration and quality of the Inca domination was linked by the authors of the 16th century with a justification of the Spanish conquest, but also because the chroniclers were not in a position to collect all the extant versions in the Andes, from the diverse populations that lived there, and they therefore mainly favored the Cusco version. Even when many of them gathered their data from outside of Cusco, they organized it within the framework of the "official history" proffered by the authors of the first chronicles, and successively repeated and broadened.

When, from the second half of the last century, adventurers and scholars became involved in archaeology and began more systematic studies into Andean antiquities, a new stage was initiated in which archaeology opened the horizons of life before the Incas. In the 20th century, the archaeologists' efforts were crowned with multiple conclusions which not only explained the brevity of the Incas' dominion, but also allowed a differentiation among the distinct moments of a long Andean trajectory, whose most ancient evidence speaks of hunters and gatherers who lived in the Andes around 10,000 years ago—the Lauricocha and Moche—and which even points back several thousand years earlier.

Archaeologists have named the Inca period the "late horizon" or "Inca horizon", also maintaining the classic name of the Inca Empire or *Tawantinsuyu*. The term "horizon" indicated a period in which the diverse Andean populations were related through a central power or through recognized cultural patterns extending throughout the region.

Today, we can appreciate that the moment when the Incas appeared, in the 15th century of our era, there was in the Andes a totality—whose numbers and territorial reach are still hard to define—of ethnic groups with varying grades of political organization, among whom the Chimor, on the northern coast of present day Peru, stood out. There, agriculture with irrigation moving large quantities of water had been developed and was supplying a significant population; now famous urban centers such as Chan Chan had been built, which covered a wide area and was home to a population estimated at between 20,000 and 30,000 inhabitants. The abundant archaeological information about this zone has allowed numerous findings about the art and symbols, from which it has been deduced that there was a centralized, theocratic government and a political organization which collided with that of the expanding Incas through long wars which the classical chroniclers related based on information predominantly from Cusco.

In the mountains of northern and central Peru there were numerous ethnic groups which did not reach the same levels of organization as Chimor and which were not greatly celebrated in the chronicles, which were more concerned with the way in which the Incas had conquered them. The Huancas of the Mantaro Valley and the Chancas of Huancavelica and Ayacucho were visible exceptions, documented to a greater degree than other groups. The latter were mentioned frequently for a famous conflict which they had with the Incas at the beginning of the Inca expansion, in the period attributed to the *Inca* Pachacuti. The former, together with other groups from the northern Andes, were described with a certain detail during the tales of the Inca conquests and, in addition, were amply documented by the Spaniards during the period of the conquest. Another thing occurred with the chronicles regarding the region of Quito, identified by some chroniclers as a "kingdom" belatedly conquered by the Incas, and which reached a standing of its own when, in the final moments of the *Tawantinsuyu* there was a war between the two aspirants to power: Huáscar and Atahuallpa, identified respectively with Cusco and Quito.

At the same time, the information in the chronicles highlighted other domains or "kingdoms", using the terminology in vogue in the European literature of the time, which had been incorporated into the *Tawantinsuyu* during its expansion. The case of Chincha, on the central coast of present day Peru, is perhaps the most notable, and its importance has been mentioned, as much in relation to its large population as because the *curaca* of Chincha was found in Cajamarca accompanying Atahuallpa in the moments when he was taken prisoner by Francisco Pizarro's band. In the southern Andes, around Lake Titicaca, there were other Aymara-speaking groups, among whom the Lupaqa, Hatuncolla and Pacaxe stood out, extensively documented in colonial papers, and also other important groups to be found spread across the extensive area of Charcas, towards the southeast along the Bolivian *altiplano*, the north of Chile and northern Argentina.

All these groups and many more, detailed today by archaeology and colonial documentation, taken together, constitute what archaeologists called the "late intermediate period" or "regional states", a sphere that also includes the early Incas of Cusco and which took place chronologically between 1100 A.D. and 1400 A.D. The ethnographic information which complements the colonial documentation has allowed us to draw new conclusions regarding the characteristics of life in those pre-Inca times.

Prior to all of the above there was an era of Andean interrelation— between the years 800 A.D. and 1100 A. D.—occupied by *Tiawanaku* and *Wari*. The center of the former was located in the region southeast of Lake Titicaca and of the latter in the mountains of Ayacucho. Both centers were identified with great urban conglomerations of the same names. Tiawanaku was known from the first moments of the Spanish invasion and figured repeatedly in the chronicles as a ruined and mysterious city; as the discipline of archaeology developed it was discovered that its antiquity was greater than that of the Incas and it was even thought that it had been another, earlier empire, even though it was thought that its excessive age and subsequent decline had led to an Andean migration towards the north, from which had arisen Inca Cusco. But the most recent archaeological studies show that Tiawanaku did not extend along the coast and mountains of present day Peru, rather just towards the south of Cusco and that, therefore, the coherent development that could be detected in the north of this region can be identified with Wari. During this period, it is believed there was a political unification, with specifically expansionist or militaristic characteristics, identified first as the Tiawanaku Empire and later also as the Wari Empire. This period is also known as the "medium horizon" in line with the theory that explained the development of the Andes through a series of successive, merging horizons with intermediate periods.

One of the most interesting points of this period is the urban organization and the possibility that many of the roads now known as Inca may have come from this period. As an example of the former, the early period of Chan Chan should be noted, as well as the classic Wari urban center in Ayacucho, although the former reached its greatest expression in a later period. Even if the militaristic nature of its expansion can be proven in this period, it is visible that in this period there was a great uniformity of criteria in different parts of the Andes, which range from the patterns of construction to, possibly, the standardization of ways of using economic resources and human energy. All this has favored the hypothesis of a centralist and expansive political organization during this period.

Before Wari-Tiawanaku there was another period that ran between the 1st and 8th centuries A.D. which has been called the "early intermediate period" or "regional cultures" to differentiate it from the unifying horizons previously mentioned. During this period many cultures developed, with the Moche (Mochica) on the northern coast of current day Peru, Cajamarca and Recuay in the northern sierra, Lima on the central coast, Ayacucho and Huarpa in the central sierra, and Nasca on the southern coast all standing out. In the southern Andes, there were also several previous, local stages of Tiawanaku. The groups and organizations of this period are generally labeled in line with the current or colonial geographical names, given the absence of any type of oral or ethnographic information—with the exception of a few partial, linguistic testimonies—and including the information from the period of the chroniclers. For this period of Andean life, archaeology has also provided fundamental findings, although it appears more difficult to draw from these any coherent conclusions comparable to those from the late intermediate period given that we do not have similar sources of ethnographic or documental information.

Before the early intermediate period there was the "early horizon", "Chavín horizon" or "formative", although this last term is chronologically broader, as it covers, *grosso modo*, the 1,500 years prior to our era, whereas Chavín, strictly speaking, had a shorter duration. Chavín gave its name to this period of Andean life. Located in the Huaylas Valley, its nuclear scope was on the ceremonial complex that bears its name, whose study comprises a milestone in the history of Peruvian archaeology. It was barely known until this century, despite the fact that in the chronicles there were references regarding its location and in the 19th century it was visited several times and some of its principal monuments and stone sculptures were described. It was thought at one time that Chavín had been a first form of state organization and expansionary characteristics were even ascribed to it. However, another theory appears more correct, one which considers it the best known example of a level of development in Andean culture with generalized agriculture. Nevertheless, we know very little about its social organization, except for some comparative and generic deductions.

Between the time of Chavín (around 1500 B.C.) and the 10,000 years of archaeological evidence in the Andes, a temporal space which contemporary research is tending to extend, there developed a long history of Andean man, from his earliest beginnings, when he arrived from the north in the central Andean region, until the appearance of the high cultures in the region. Its description goes beyond the scope of this book.

The history of man in the Andes is long and it should be understood that the Incas did not represent a rupture in this process, rather, that their existence was made possible by the ample, prior experience. The Incas probably therefore offered little original in the Andes, although that does not in any way diminish the importance of their history; they were the only Andean organization about which we have generous historical testimony regarding the way in which it was established, the lines along which it was ruled, especially the structuring of its economy, about which we know more and more thanks to the concurrence of various disciplines. Today we can see in the Incas just one moment in the long Andean continuum, notable over a far greater duration than simply the period preceding and following the Spanish invasion of the 16ᵗʰ century. It is also certain the Incas brought Andean forms of organization to new levels that had previously been inconceivable, making the most of their historical experience; this can be best appreciated in the forms of extensive, mass production, which were based on extremes of reciprocity and redistribution as basic characteristics of the Andean economy and social relations. None of this could have happened without conflicts, but it also required a certain, basic consensus, reachable through the common experience traditionally accepted by the Andean population. Inca organization has given rise to the formulation of various retrospective utopias, with some seeing in the *Tawantinsuyu* an excellent form of primitive communism or a socialist empire of the past. It has also been characterized as a totalitarian and enslaving organization. All this reflects, perhaps, more than is appropriate, namely the academic necessity to demonstrate specific hypotheses just as Eurocentric as those which shaped the writing of the chronicles of the 16ᵗʰ century.

Chapter II
The Origin of the Incas

There are many theories regarding the origin of the Incas, from the myths collected by the chroniclers of the 16th century to the modern explanations and hypotheses proposed by specialists, even though this has ceased to be a principal theme in the research of recent years as the subject has stopped being the motivation for passionate specialization as was the case in the last century and the beginning of this century.

The myths of Cusco and contemporary archaeology coincide in indicating the Cusco area as the place of origin of the *Tawantinsuyu* ("the four parts of the world" or "all the world"), now known as the *Inca Empire* thanks to the chroniclers of the 16th century. In Cusco there is evidence of a lengthy human occupation and going back one thousand years before Christ there was already agriculture. Regarding the development of Cusco prior to the 15th century, we know very little with certainty beyond the identification of ceramics and architectonic forms, which both predate the classic Inca styles. It should be noted, nevertheless, that before the rise of the *Tawantinsuyu*, there existed diverse ethnic groups, some of which have been better identified than others. Among these the Ayarmaca stand out, and they have been better studied than the other groups mentioned in the chronicles, such as the Alcavizas, Sahuasiray, etc. Little is known about them even though they frequently appear in the chronicles and other colonial texts as peoples who used altars neighboring Cusco or even inside the actual city. The mythical versions mention them, differentiating them from the Incas, who are considered an independent group. There also persists a confusing panorama in this regard, given that the term *Inca* is often used to designate personally the rulers as well as certain relatives, who are generally known as *panaqa*. Usually, the *panaqas* were distinguished from "normal" groups of relatives, known as *ayllu*. In Cusco, there lived diverse *ayllus* linked to the *Incas*.

When the chroniclers researched the origins of the Incas, they received information arranged according to Andean categories; firstly, they heard tales regarding the origin of the world, and subsequently, regarding the origin of the Incas, which was their point of special interest given that the particular situation of the Inca "dynasty" affected important questions such as the "legitimacy" of the Spanish conquest. Naturally, the chroniclers took this information for fables. Nevertheless, this is the thematic order in which the notions of the origins appear: Firstly, that of the world itself, the ordering of the world, and then the "origin" of the Incas. At least, that is the way it was presented by those chroniclers who wrote in more detail about the subject. The subject was certainly dealt with by those who wrote before 1550, even though their works were published later. But the first chroniclers who appear to have written with some basis in the oral tradition of Cusco were Pedro Cieza de León, who wrote around 1550, and Juan de Betanzos, who finished his work in 1551. We will deal here with Betanzos' text not just because he resided for a long period in Cusco and married a woman from the Cusco elite, but also because he learnt the *runasimi* well enough to act as an official interpreter.

Only now that we know the entire text of the *Narration of the Incas* by Juan de Betanzos, can we see that the first pages of his work summarize and reproduce a myth of the ordering of the world and the origin of man. He subsequently deals with the origin of the Incas. These subject are dealt with in the third and fourth chapters of his work.

Summarizing Betanzos' text, and after the chronicler indicated how Wiraqocha had "ordered" the world (*Wiraqocha* can be understood as a divinity model, with diverse manifestations which may correspond to each part of the Andean world, as will be seen later) and intended that man emerged from below the earth, four couples rose from a cave in Pacaritampu: Ayar Cache-Mama Guaco, Ayar Oche [Uchu]-Cara, Ayar Auca-Ragua Ocllo, y Ayar Manco-Mama Ocllo. Each of these carried a golden "halberd", called *Tupa Yauri*, wore fine clothes with gold borders (*cumbi*) and wore around their necks some bags, also made of *cumbi,* with catapults made from the sinews of camelids. The women used gold jewellery, for example brooches or clasps, known as *tupu*. From Pacaritampu, which the chronicler translates as "house of production", they went to a mountain named Guanacaure and its lower slopes were used to sow potatoes. From the summit of Guanacaure, Ayar Cache hurled several stones using his catapult, cracking four mountains and making four fissures in them. Following this demonstration of strength, his companions decided to rid themselves of him and they all returned to Pacaritampu under the pretext of collecting some objects of gold that they had left in the cave from which they had originally come. Once there, Ayar Cache entered the cave and the others covered the mouth of the cave with a great slab, leaving Ayar Cache trapped inside, trying in vain to escape. After this, the others returned to Guanacaure, where they stayed for a year, after which they moved to another stream called Matagua, closer to Cusco. From there they descended to the valley of Cusco where Alcaviza lived with a group of 30 Indians. They left Ayar Oche in Guanacaure, "transformed into an idol" after flying into the sky to talk with "his father" the Sun.

The versions of Betanzos and other other chroniclers presented the Ayar as "brothers". Ayar Oche brought an instruction from the Sun to change the name of Ayar Manco to Manco Cápac. Finally this last one, along with his last "brother", Ayar Auca, and the four women, arrived in Cusco, where they established themselves after negotiating with Alcaviza, who accepted their character as "children of the Sun". They then sowed maize.

This story about the Ayar is also told by other chroniclers, with some small variations. Pedro Cieza de León, for example, who finished the second part of his *Chronicle of Peru* at approximately the same time as Betanzos, as well as Inca Garcilaso de la Vega, both have a version of this story. The story of the Ayar appears, both in Betanzos and Cieza de León, as the oldest or perhaps "most genuine" expression that the inhabitants of Cusco told about their earliest origins. Each couple could be assimilated to the four parts in which Cusco and the world was divided. Each one of these had been mentioned in an earlier myth that was retold by the chroniclers, which dealt with the creation of the world by Wiraqocha. It is certain that the world "creation" could cause an error here; it does not refer to the Judeo-Christian creation, which conceives of the world being created from nothing by a divinity, but rather it deals with the "ordering of the world", which was previously in a chaotic situation. The myth links the "founders" of Cusco with the sacred metals, such as gold. It also associates them with specific crops; potatoes, coca, chili peppers and maize, and it mentions that Ayar Manco received his new name, Manco Cápac, at the disposition of the solar deity, although this is only mentioned towards the end of the story. From the final part of the story, it can also be deduced that it was two of the male siblings who arrived in Cusco, a fact which may be related to the two parts into which Cusco is divided, *Hanin* and *urin*. Recent research has attempted to clarify the internal structures of this myth of the "brothers" Ayar, exemplified here in the version of Juan de Betanzos and repeated with variations by other chroniclers. It should also be remembered that the version of Betanzos benefits on the one hand from the prestige of being one of the oldest and, on the other, specifically from the condition of bilingualism of its author.

The first part of the myth lays out an itinerary towards Cusco. It is only after sowing potatoes and the "elimination" of Ayar Cache, trapping him in the original cave, thus returning him to the subsoil-womb, that the connection with "the father-Sun" is produced, on the mountain of Gaunacaure, when Ayar Oche is transformed into a stone after having "gone to the sky" and returned converted into a solar messenger who gives Ayar Manco his new name. Only after establishing themselves in Cusco do the surviving Ayar sow maize, with seeds carried from the cave of Pacaritampu. One can appreciate here an order, possibly even a hierarchy, of products: potatoes, coca, chili peppers, maize. This may also tell us something about the basic resources of the area, which are important as they signify a visible, agricultural complementarity, given that each of these comes from a distinct ecological zone.

It should be added that in other versions, such as that of Cieza de León, there are variations not just in the "events" of the myth but also in the order and name of the characters. For example, according to Cieza, it is Ayar *Cachi,* trapped in the cave, who appears before his siblings as an envoy from the Sun on the summit of Guanacaure. However, the differing accounts do not lead us to dismiss the version of Betanzos, given that both versions are probably based on the same source.

Another type of myth about the origin of the Incas is the one spread by Inca Garcilaso de la Vega, whose *Royal Commentaries of the Incas* were published belatedly in 1609. In reality, Garcilaso published three versions in his work: One of these coincides in general terms with that of Betanzos and, apparently, Garcilaso only used sources from Cusco. A second version mentions a deluge and, discarding the prolixity of this version which he considered to be a fable, the chronicler solemnly indicates that "…when the waters had ceased, a man appeared in Tiawanaku, who arrived in Cusco at midday, and was so powerful that he divided the world in four parts and he gave them to four men who he called kings; the first was called Manco Cápac, the segund Colla, the third Tocay and the fourth Pinahua." Each one of these kings corresponded with one of the four parts of Cusco and the world. It adds that Manco Cápac went from Tiawanaku to Cusco and initiated the *Tawantinsuyu*. Interestingly, Garcilaso attributed the first version, that of the Ayar mentioned here, to the residents of the north and east of Cusco, and the last story, regarding the four kings, to those from the south and west of the city. As we will see, the first two areas correspond to the *Hanin* sectors and the other two areas to the *urin* sectors of the city.

However, Garcilaso de la Vega gave a privileged role in his chronicle to a different story, one which has spread greatly, as much for the way it appears in this celebrated chronicle as for the fact that the work of this author has been widely distributed in various languages ever since it first appeared.

According to the version of Inca Garcilaso, the Sun god made Manco Cápac and Mama Ocllo, a married couple who were also brother and sister, emerge from Lake Titicaca. The couple had received divine instruction to head towards the north carrying a rod of gold, which they were to periodically place in the earth. When the rod sank, it would signal that the divinity had chosen the place where the couple should establish themselves. This happened in Cusco and there Manco Cápac and Mama Ocllo installed themselves. They then told the people of their solar origin and showed them how to sow maize and weave, among other civilizing activities. In this version, Guanacaure, already know to the reader from the previous tale of the Ayar, also figures as the place where the gold rod sank. Elements from the previous version can also be found in this one, such as Guanacaure, which appears in both myths as the place where the "solar revelation" occurs. It is possible that this last account of Garcilaso has been elaborated to give greater consistency to the origin of the Incas, establishing consecration of the original couple and eliminating the others. This may well be a belated revision of the original account, as Garcilaso himself indicates, preparing it for the elite of Cusco.

In all the accounts presented here, it can be appreciated that Manco Cápac or Ayar Manco appears linked with the cultivation of maize. It is worth underlining that the region of Cusco produces maize of great quality, something for which it is known in various parts of the Andes, even in our times. A good part of this maize was produced in the Urubamba valley, where there were numerous terraces for cultivation, commonly known as *andenes*, including some that were circular, such as the one at Moray, which may have served as a laboratory for experimenting with the cultivation of maize, given that the terraces could reproduce different climatic conditions, specifically temperature, corresponding to different zones and altitudes of the valley. Manco Cápac appears in general in the chronicles as an archetype, who designs or models the biographies of his successors, until the appearance of Pachacuti, the ninth *Inca* in most accounts, who "remodeled the world", transforming himself into a new archetype for the final *Incas*. Pachacuti is also presented in the chronicles as the "son of Manco Cápac" which makes him "his equal". For this reason, the subsequent Incas refer to Pachacuti in the same way as earlier Incas did to Manco Cápac.

The Early Organization of Cucso and the Formation of the Tawantinsuyu

Generally, the chronicles of the 16th and 17th centuries assumed a first "dynasty" of Inca "kings", which they refer to as *urin* Cusco. From Inca Roca, a change took place which led to the formation of a new dynasty known as *hanan* Cusco (see figure 1). The former has been identified with "lower Cusco" and the latter with "upper Cusco", the two halves that gave their names to these dynasties. The chronicles tell us that each *Inca,* on taking power, originated a *panaqa* or kinship group comprised of his descendants and other relatives. The accounts of the successive dynasties has been debated by various specialists who have proposed distinct forms of organization, based in some cases on the situation which research into the *curacas* or Andean ethnic chiefs has made evident; all the chiefdoms had dual structures of authority, which, thanks to the Spanish invasion, were transformed into two parallel lines of descendants when the *curacas* were obliged to demonstrate that they were "legitimate" sons of their predecessors. This applied both to the *hanan* and *urin.*

The genealogy of the Incas, referenced by the chroniclers, divided in dynasties can be seen in figure 1. There have been various proposals about how best to order them: a) Taking into account the change the chronicles relate happened in the times attributed to the Inca Pachacuti, who clearly appears as the instigator of a new phase in the genealogy of the Incas of Cusco, initiating a great territorial expansion of the *Tawantinsuyu*, and is represented as a new architect who designed the role of the subsequent *Incas*, in the same way that Manco Cápac did for those prior to Pachacuti; b) In the form of parallel dynasties, based on some of the information presented in the chronicles, and also using corresponding notions of dualism in Inca authority, visible in the Andean *curacas*. In line with information from some chroniclers, the Jesuit José de Acosta for example, some have postulated a diarchy instead of a monarchy. This formulation is represented in figure 2. Even though this theory would mainly affect the structure of power in Inca Cusco, it would not affect the classical images which place the beginning of the great expansion of the *Tawantinsuyu* in the period attributed to the Inca Pachacuti. This latest theory is currently being debated, given that its formulation does not yet include a reprocessing of the accounts of the chronicles despite being based in the negation of an Inca history as narrated by the chroniclers. Without any doubt, this will be an interesting and contentious subject for a long time to come.

FIGURE 1

Urin Cusco	Hanan Cusco
Manco Cápac	Inca Roca
Sinchi Roca	Yaguar Guaca
Lloque Yupanqui	Wiracocha
Mayta Cápac	Pachacuti
Cápac Yupanqui	Amaru Inca Yupanqui
	Túpac Inca Yupanqui
	Guayna Cápac
	Guascar
	Atahualpa

FIGURE 2

	Manco Cápac	
Hanan		**Urin**
Inca Roca	1	Sinchi Roca
Yaguar Guaca	2	Cápac Yupanqui
Viracocha	3	Lloque Yupanqui
Inca Yupanqui		
Pachacuti	4	Mayta Cápac
Túpac Yupanqui	5	Tarco Guaman
Túpac Yupanqui II	6	Hijo del anterior
Guayna Cápac	7	Tambo Mayta, Don Juan
Guáscar	8	Tambo Mayta, Don Juan

Source: Duviols 1980.

We know very little about the early organization of Inca Cusco beyond what the chronicles tell us. It is noticeable that the accounts of the chronicles are highly influenced by the characteristics and categories that governed the elaboration of history in 16th century Europe. It is also understandable that the chroniclers used models from the historic literature of their times or that was common in their days; the *Commentaries* of the wars of the Gauls, the civil war of Julius Caesar, or the work of Thucydides, etc., served as literary models for many of the chronicles and the same thing also happened with medieval and renaissance annals and stories, widely used as models. The chroniclers could not escape the temptation to project the European experience onto the new lands which they were beginning to discover. For this reason, many European mythical themes and some Mediterranean ones appear in the chronicles as certain facts.

In the same way, the 16th century authors projected the mythological monsters which inhabited the edges of the world in the mediaeval and classical texts onto the Americas they were discovering, and in doing so indicated the places classical mythology and mediaeval Europe considered important. Biblical paradise was thus located in the Americas, as well as the mythical kingdom of the Amazons (whose queen, Califia, gave her name to California) and whose generic name was given to South America's great river. The same thing occurred with the lost cities of gold and the mines of King Solomon. The European chroniclers debated whether Peru was the biblical Ophir and many authors concerned themselves with investigating whether the inhabitants of the Americas were descendants of ancient Mediterranean migrants.

We do not have concrete reasons for asserting that Cusco immediately after the formation and expansion of the *Tawantinsuyu* was very different from the ethnic groups of Peru's southern Andes in the first half of the 15th century. A complementary ecological system must have functioned which gave access to multiple agricultural resources (there will be a more detailed description of this in the next chapter). The presence of four such resources in the origin myths of Cusco (potatoes, coca, chili peppers and maize) explains this as they each have distinct ecological origins. The valleys neighboring Cusco were rich in maize and potatoes, with distinct varieties in the nearby highlands. Coca was produced on lower lands, further down the valley of the Urubamba River, and chili peppers nearby. To a large degree, this confluence of resources, along with moderate amounts of Andean livestock such as alpacas and llamas, was able to sustain the economy of early Cusco.

If we follow the accounts of the chronicles, there is one moment prior to the great expansion of Cusco that should be emphasized; the war against the Chancas. They lived in the region located to the north of Cusco, beyond the Apurímac River, between the current departments of Ayacucho and Huancavelica. As we saw in the first chapter, the Chancas belonged to the "regional states" that existed between the predominance of the Wari and that of the *Tawantinsuyu*. The chronicles mention the Chancas as hardened warriors, but always in relation to the *Tawantinsuyu* of the Incas, given that the oral traditions gathered by the chroniclers generally came from Cusco and its vicinity. For this reason, we know about the Chancas almost solely through their relationship with Cusco and their disputes with the Incas. The same issue applies to the other Andean ethnic groups.

There are two other accounts which relate the contacts and conflicts between the Incas and the Chancas. The first tells us that in the times of *Inka* Wiraqocha—although authors such as Inca Garcilaso de la Vega attribute the events to the time of his predecessor Yahuar Huaraca—the Chancas, led by Asto Huaraca and Tomay Huaraca, invaded Cusco. The Inca Wiraqocha abandoned the city, taking refuge in the neighboring Yucay Valley, along with his son and heir, Inca Urcon. The chronicles describe the violence of the Chanca invasion and the defeat of the Inca armies. Abandoned by Inca Wiraqocha, Cusco was occupied by the victorious Chancas, who ransacked and destroyed it. But Wiraqocha had another son, named Inca Yupanqui, who had been "banished" from Cusco. This son had a vision in which the Sun appeared and ordered him to go to Cusco and expel the Chancas. That is what Yupanqui did and in Cusco the stones turned into soldiers to confront the Incas' enemies, defeating them. After beating them, Yupanqui went to look for his father, Wiraqocha, who rejected the triumph as it had not been wrought by Urcon. This son confronted Yupanqui and was vanquished amid a series of events described in the chronicles as a product of palace intrigues. Recognized as the *Inca*, and finally having the support of his famous father, Yupanqui changed his name for that of *Pachacuti*, a term which has been generically translated as "he who renews the world", and dedicated himself to rebuilding Cusco and reforming its structures.

Another singular version of this story is provided by Pedro Gutiérrez de Santa Clara, a chronicler widely known for his writings about the wars that took place among the Spaniards after the invasion of the 16ᵗʰ century. His famous *History of the Civil Wars of Peru* was written towards the end of the 16ᵗʰ century or at the start of the 17ᵗʰ century. This author's account is based on an assumption distinct from that of most of the other chroniclers of the history of Peru: The Incas originated around Lake Titicaca, but they established themselves in Hatun Colla, northeast of the Lake, rather than Cusco. The author describes the lives of the first Incas in the traditionally recognized list, who began their conquests from Hatun Colla. During the government of Wiraqocha, "two brothers named Guamán Guaraza and Aucos Guaraza rose up against him, the *Inca*, and went against him from the province of Andahuaylas, where they were lords and took the lands of the *Inca*." Here also arose Pachacuti, the younger of the sons of the Inca Wirqocha, who defeated the Chancas.

After this, Pachacuti left Hatun Colla in search of conquests towards the north, confronting the *curaca* of Cusco, who had many followers. Pachacuti won but was wounded and died. But his death was kept secret and it was said that the Sun had taken him. In the chronicler's text, Pachacuti dies in Urcos and does not arrive in Cusco to occupy the city. However, Gutiérrez de Santa Clara states that until this moment "they were not called the *masters* of Cusco, nor of the other towns of those provinces, but rather *curacas*, which simply means *master*." But as the successor of Pachacuti, Tupa Inca Yupanqui, arrived to finally enter Cusco, he ordered that those who had arrived with him should be known as *Incas*.

There is a noticeable difference between the two versions. In the first, the *Inca* leaves Cusco to fight the Chancas. In the second, the *Inca* defeats the Chancas and then vanquishes the *curaca* of Cusco, thus occupying the city. The two versions coincide in indicating that the Incas came from Lake Titicaca, given that the first of these accounts is rooted in the origin myths of Cusco and the second confirms it implicitly. Both versions differentiate explicitly regarding the foundation or occupation of Cusco.

There is no doubt that the first version proceeds directly from the oral tradition of Cusco, gathered by the chroniclers. The second, however, can be easily identified with an account from outside of Cusco. The visible discrepancy can be attributed to this, although it should also be emphasized that chronicles written by Andeans, such as Felipe Guamán Poma de Ayala or Juan de Santa Cruz Pachacuti Yamqui Salcamaygua, do not discuss the ancient identification of the Incas with Cusco, in line with the general view of the chronicles. However, a major problem should be acknowledged; there are grave and well-founded doubts about whether Pedro Gutiérrez de Santa Clara was really in Peru, given that his presence was documented in Mexico, from where he hailed. The provenance of his information regarding Peru can be debated, although it is evident that the people of Mexico and Peru were in constant communication during that period, and many of those who left Peru during the civil wars among the *conquistadores* (a subject which Gutiérrez de Santa Clara treats in great detail) passed through Mexico before heading to Spain. There is no certainty, therefore, regarding the provenance of the information of this chronicler and, although it is known that the authors of the era copied each other, nothing allows us to think that the summary of the history of the Incas that Gutiérrez de Santa Clara offers might be correct, or at least no more or less correct than others.

The only thing that can be said with certainty regarding the account of Gutiérrez de Santa Clara is that recent studies allow us to affirm that his history of the Incas is a skillful modification of the text of another chronicler, Diego Fernández, known as Palentino, who published his chronicle in 1571. This further reduces the possibility that Gutiérrez de Santa Clara could have provided an alternative version of Inca history.

The Inca Conquests

The chronicles attribute the conquests of a wide territory that constituted the *Tawantinsuyu* to successive *Incas*. As previously indicated, the conquests of the first *Incas* were restricted to the area neighboring Cusco. The great expansion began in the period attributed to Pachacuti, 100 years before the Spanish invasion, in the time after the invasion of the Chancas and the victory of the people of Cusco over them.

The first zone of expansion appears to have been the region of Lake Titicaca. The chroniclers relate how Inca Pachacuti—some authors say Wiraqocha—allied himself with the Lupaqa, one of the most important ethnic groups of the area, in order to defeat the powerful "king" of Hatun Colla. The texts of the chroniclers of the 16th century, repeated widely in other Spanish texts of the colonial period, emphasize the importance of this conquest, which placed the people of the Lake Titicaca region under Inca supremacy. The Inca armies then directed themselves northwards, conquering, according to the chroniclers, all the way to the central sierra, in the current administrative department of Junín. The chronicles thus relate that during a certain period the combined efforts of Pachacuti and his successor, Tupa Inca Yupanqui, permitted the northwards expansion of the dominions of the *Tawantinsuyu* along the coast and into the

45

mountains, until arriving in the region of Quito. Subsequently, Tupa Inca Yupanqui managed to conquer as far south as Tucumán and central Chile. Equally, the chronicles attribute the final conquests in the Andean zone to Huayna Cápac (see the map of these conquests, as related by the chroniclers).

But the information in the chronicles is not uniform, especially when checked against the most local descriptions provided by important sets of documentation, such as the *Geographic Relation of the Indies*, administrative visits and other accounts which refer to specific ethnic groups. We can obtain, therefore, different versions, not just regarding the general tendency or course of the expeditions but also relative to the progressive occupation of territory. There are two types of problems regarding this subject: Some refer to the notion of territoriality and, in consequence, are related to the occupation of space; others are concerned with the sequence of the conquests as provided by the accounts in the chronicles.

The first problem has been analyzed in the research of recent years and there have been various developments which allow a better understanding of the notion of space. There has been a symbolic vision of space in the Andes for a long time (which will be dealt with in the chapter on cosmovision). But, since the times in which the chroniclers wrote, an image of space has predominated that dealt with territory organized politically into "provinces" corresponding to different ethnic groups mentioned in the chronicles and who, in fact, viewed the Inca expansion in accordance with the very provinces that they themselves had previously conquered. In this way, the general view of the chronicles leaves the impression that these provinces existed prior to the formation of the *Tawantinsuyu* and that they corresponded to each of the ethnic groups, which equally pre-existed as political organizations. This does not appear to be true in all cases and, in the extreme, might correspond to a division realized during the *Tawantinsuyu*.

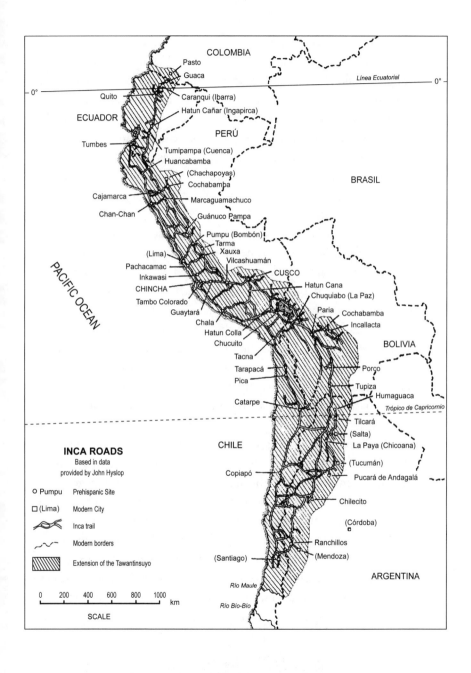

INCA ROADS
Based in data
provided by John Hyslop

○ Pumpu   Prehispanic Site

□ (Lima)   Modern City

〜〜   Inca trail

〜〜   Modern borders

▨   Extension of the Tawantinsuyo

0   200   400   600   800   1000
                                  km

SCALE

Research in recent years has suggested variations of this notion of territoriality, especially the work of John V. Murra on the ethnic groups of Lake Titicaca and of the central zone of present day Peru (Huánuco). From this we can deduce that the Andean people saw territory not as continuous units but as a whole of ecologically differentiated zones in which it was possible to access diverse resources. The population of just one ethnic group was able therefore to be distributed over a very wide area compared to other ethnic groups. This occurred, for example, in the Lake Titicaca region, and is the case of the Lupaqa.

These people lived in a region around the southeast of the Lake, but they controlled areas located a great distance from their actual nucleus, where some of the population lived permanently (in reality, small groups of people, such as *mitmaqkuna*) but larger groups dedicated to sowing and harvesting (such as *mittani*) also travelled to these areas at specific times of the year. A discontinuous territory was thus configured, where the Lupaqa controlled zones that were differentiated ecologically and up to 15 or 20 days distance by foot. The extremes of this apparently excessive range were found on the Pacific coast and the lower areas on the east of the *altiplano* of Peru and Bolivia. The intermediate zones were not occupied by the Lupaqa and the "peripheral" areas could be simultaneously occupied by other ethnic groups. They were, in fact, multi-ethnic. Other groups from the same region of the Lake, and the *altiplano* in general, used similar systems to control multiple ecologies and achieve the complementarity that assured the provision of different resources.

This form of employing territory did not exclude the neighboring communities of Lake Titicaca. Rather, we find them in other regions, such as Huánuco, where the Chupaychu made similar use of zones situated at varying distances, although these distances were much less than those existing in the lake region. It appears that the control of resources from distinct, neighboring and ecologically differentiated regions was a generalized practice in the Andes. This notion necessarily collided with the image of "provinces" or continuous, isolated territories in which each ethnic group exercised uncontested control.

This situation was even more complex inside the nuclear areas of the different ethnic groups, as evidenced in the case of the Lupaqa, given that each of the distinct "towns" described in the Spanish documentation of the 16th century controlled varied spaces, distributed in the same nuclear zone and territories previously apparently belonging to each of the seven peoples or "administrative units" registered in the Lupaqa area. In the same way, it can be appreciated that an *ayllu* or kinship group could be distributed in various zones and, especially as a consequence of the Spanish invasion, in different *reducciones* (the name given to the towns organized by the Spaniards to redistribute the Andean population according to European criteria). In this way, the territory of an ethnic unit was not constituted by a continuous space, but by a collection of ecologically delimited spaces which could be found at varying distances.

The second problem is regarding the chronology of the conquests, which appear in the chronicles as an organic sequence. On a more detailed analysis, we can appreciate that some of the *Incas* were conquering zones whose conquest had been attributed to their ancestors. This happened with one of the last *Incas*, Huayna Cápac, who, in some chronicles, features conquering lands very near to Cusco itself. The chronicles appear to be dealing with an account of a ritual conquest.

Checking some of the chroniclers, for example Cieza de León, Sarmiento de Gamboa or Cabello Balboa, it is possible to appreciate that since Pachacuti, Inca conquests are always manifested as a series of expeditions which moved clockwise, with each one leaving from and returning to Cusco. This appears to fit more with the account of a conquest ritual than with the history of real conquest. The chroniclers leave news about how each *Inca* represented accounts of the glorious deeds of his ancestors as part of the ceremonies for his accession to power. From this, close relationships between history and representation were generated, manifested in many cases as a form of theater; we have already mentioned the colonial and contemporary use of dramatic representations which transmit information regarding the past.

It is very possible, therefore, that the chroniclers took from the Andean populace the corresponding accounts of ritual representations and not stories in the occidental sense. This is better explained by the fact that the chronicles' accounts of the Inca conquests present a stable order with successive conquests in a clockwise direction, as already indicated, giving the impression of a spiral movement. This seems to be more the account of a ritual than of a series of expeditions of successive rulers.

Although the chronicles prefer to highlight the conquests as military achievements, at the same time they inform us of distinct and not exclusive mechanisms. The expansion of the *Tawantinsuyu* can be seen as the establishment of a series of reciprocal and redistributory relationships. The chronicles tell us that the march of the Inca armies was accompanied by a considerable number of porters who carried clothing, generally of wool, and other important resources, for example coca or *mullu (Spondylus,* a type of oyster shell greatly appreciated for ritual offerings). These goods were distributed by the *Inca* as one of his first acts, which even replaced conflict with an "alliance" between the ethnic group and the Inca *Tawantinsuyu.* This "present" can thus be interpreted as a form of initiating a redistributive relationship. Of course, that did not necessarily exclude compulsion and allows us to understand the subsequent obligation of the ethnic groups incorporated into the *Tawantinsuyu* to regularly provide manual labor for defined periods of times, *mitta*, allowing the *Tawantinsuyu* in turn to generate a new, redistributable surplus.

It is through this lens of established relationships that we must view the life of the *Tawantinsuyu* and its rapid expansion in the Andes. And it is thus more noticeable that Inca political organization used old mechanisms of redistribution widely employed over a long time prior to the Incas, and that these in turn allowed the Incas' rapid expansion. Often, the chronicles and other documents tell us about the marriages between the *Inca* and the daughters or sisters of Andean *curacas*, as well as the links between those *curacas* and the women of the family of the ruler of Cusco. This type of marriage-alliance was closely linked with the establishment of reciprocal and, in consequence, redistributive obligations. If the gifts referred to earlier set the beginning of a new relationship, marriages of this type clearly established a set of relationships that articulated the life of the *Tawantinsuyu* of the Incas, framing the links of Cusco with other ethnic groups. The outlines were not the same everywhere and the *Tawantinsuyu* knew how to vary its demands in order to adapt to the different regions and ethnic groups. Nevertheless, distributive notions had priority in all areas, including the provision of manual labor and the redistribution of specific goods by Cusco.

Chapter III
The Inca Economy

Much has been said of the economic organization of the *Tawantinsuyu*. Beyond talking directly about the justice or injustice of Cusco's political domination of the Andes, the chroniclers of the 16th century presented the achievements of the Incas as notable in economic terms. This translated into a just distribution of riches, abundant agricultural and livestock production, and the considerable organization that made possible the construction of an enormous system of storage spread across the length of the extensive territory dominated by the *Tawantinsuyu*, thanks to the large network of paths which has rightfully attracted the attention of all those concerned with the Andes. The chroniclers certainly highlighted the efficiency of this administration, often insisting that it had banished poverty, avoided hunger and given each person a correct remuneration for his work. Authors of the 19th and 20th centuries maintained these almost utopian assertions and even considered the Incas of Cusco as one of the greatest examples of primitive communism or socialism, identifying both as ideals of distributive justice.

In the Andes, an economy without money, markets or trade functioned. Nor was there tribute, considered in its traditional form. There was, however, a regime of multiple reciprocities amid the population, thus generating an exchange based in the lending of human energy, fundamentally governed by the norms established by kinship. On the other hand, the authorities, local as well as central, received manual labor which allowed them to organize production destined to support a redistribution of broad reach.

Studying the Andean economy without taking into account kinship is impossible, given that this made reciprocity feasible. The members of an extended family, or *ayllu*, were related by multiple ritually established obligations. The reciprocities thus generated covered practically all the aspects of daily life. This has made it common that, when the economic life of the Andean population is explained, it is done in communal terms, with the community interpreted as based in the collective ownership of goods, basically land and herds of camelids. What we really find in the Andes is a community based on *work* rather than the existence of common property. It is possible that the chroniclers of the 16th century and even modern historians think in these terms given that they have not been able to shake off the Eurocentric image of property, which has such a long tradition in European history. But, if we abstract a notion of property, the problem has different characteristics; we understand, therefore, that the use of goods is linked to the social structure and kinship, on one level, and the structure of relations between ethnic groups, on another.

The information in the chronicles allows us to appreciate that in the Andes notions of wealth and poverty should be understood in a structural rather than individual form as they did not depend on the possibility of accumulation; rather, they were fundamentally rooted in access to labor produced by the relationship system. *Poor* is translated as *waqcha* in Quechua, but *waqcha* primordially means *orphan*, in other words someone without parents. The texts of Huarochirí, compiled at the end of the 16th century or the beginning of the 17th century at the initiative of the cleric Francisco de Avila, possibly constitute the most important collection of Andean myths, coming from the central sierra of present-day Peru. When they speak of *Huatyacuri* and attempt to explain that he is *poor*, they do so by affirming that he was only able to eat roast potatoes. As far as the economy was concerned, one of the basic characteristics of the organization of the population was the close link existing between kinship relations, reciprocity and wealth. The classic chronicles also touch upon this explanation; for example, Inca Garcilaso de la Vega transcribed in his *Royal Commentaries of the Incas* several phrases from the manuscripts of the *mestizo* Blas Valera: "...he was called rich who had children and family to help him with work in order to finish more speedily the tributary work which fell to him. And he, who did not have [family, kin] even though he might be rich in other things, was poor ..."

Since the chroniclers made such an important point of the help that the Andean population mutually provided each other, it has taken a long time for this "help," which motivated "collectivist" explanations of the Andean economy, to be more correctly interpreted. Today it is more widely understood that the absence of poverty in the pre-Hispanic Andes was thanks to the vigor of these reciprocal exchanges, which did not just consist of goods but also the use of human energy of the kinship group. The population was thus able to rely principally on the energy of their kin to achieve the most complete self-sufficiency possible. This reciprocity was exercised through the mutual lending of human energy for communal production. The chroniclers called this *ayni*, considering it a form of mutual help rather than the obligation that it was, based on kinship. Given that this guaranteed reciprocity, it can be understood that its strengthening contributed to the satisfaction of basic necessities and that its absence determined poverty, equivalent when all is said and done, to orphanhood and isolation.

The solidarity sustained by kinship was, thus, what prevented poverty in the Andes, and it led to the noted praise of the chroniclers. They explained this situation with a successful formula; the omnipotence and parallel omniscience of Inca state power was such that it was able to make up for all the needs of the population. A rigid work discipline organized by the authorities, at every tier from the Inca to the most humble functionaries of an enormous administrative machine, had made it possible to regiment large-scale production in the ample dominions of the *Tawantinsuyu* and establish at the same time the appropriate mechanisms to distribute its products among the population. The *Tawantinsuyu* thus comes across in the chronicles as a totalitarian state but also as a benefactor (forms which all totalitarianisms present in their utopian formulations) in an idealized retrospective that illuminates all its history but which clouds the creative activity of the Andean population; centuries before the *Tawantinsuyu* was founded, this population had already systematized the reciprocal and redistributive norms that made possible the long and successful formation of the Inca Empire.

Recent research has shown that the origins of Andean reciprocity are remote and difficult to clarify. It certainly appears that the chronicles and administrative writings of the 16th century refer to the past immediately prior to the Spanish invasion. It is possible to detect reciprocity functioning since the period directly prior to the invasion as well as enduring into the present, with some inevitable modifications. The Andean family organization has been better explained in recent years and we can now appreciate the close relationship that existed between the organization of kinship, centered on the *ayllu*, and the ritual ordering that governed and justified mutual lending rooted in these very kinship relationships. In general terms, we can affirm that these reciprocal relationships presumed, at the level of the *ayllu*, certain stable obligations, as well as others generated in a specific form. The former derive directly from family connections while the latter appear to function at higher levels, either through relationships established between *ayllus*, including those with a particularly long reach which could link different ethnic groups, each of which comprises diverse ayllus. In this way, we can better understand how the *ayllu* was the base on which the various levels of Andean organization rested.

The most stable reciprocity relationships within the *ayllu* appear to have functioned as deliveries of human energy but there are also many testimonies that mention deliveries of goods. However, these appear more linked to known forms of the ritual exchange of gifts, which may have coincided more with the traditional obligations of hospitality. It is possible that in exchanges of this last type predominated "raw" goods, those whose elaboration did not require a specific investment of human energy. On the other hand, for reciprocities governed solely by kinship relations, contemporary ethnographic evidence allows us to evaluate the delivery of gifts, but to a much greater degree the reciprocal exchanges of human energy destined for common supply.

The *curacas* were Andean ethnic lords; the chronicles generally referred to them as *caciques*, employing the West Indian term that was first transplanted to Mexico and then to the Andes. They were in charge of administering collective life and, among their most important functions was the regulation of exchanges of human energy. Given that the information in the chronicles of the 16th century was inevitably marked by the feudal patterns of Europe, the Andean *curacas* were presented as lords of vassals. But at the same time, like a projection of the strengthening of the centralist state of Spain at that time, the *curacas* figured in the chronicles of the 16th century as functionaries named by the *Inca*, from whom they would have received their delegated power and position. On the other hand, recent studies regarding the Andean *curaca* clearly reinforce his long preexistence before the Incas as well as the ritual condition of his position. At the same time, they confirm his essential situation as a mediator in the internal relations of the group, including that of reciprocity. But the *curaca* was also the administrator of the surplus produced by the management of communal human energy, which made possible the *redistribution* of this excess, either to complement the needs of the group or to organize the reserves necessary for periods of drought or other calamities, including war.

Reciprocity can be conceived symmetrically or asymmetrically. The former is easily understood when members of a kinship group employ collective energy for growing crops or constructing house roofs. Modern examples allow us to see the way in which this last activity causes kin to congregate for the task, each of whom can in turn demand the same service. The chronicles have sanctioned as *ayni* all forms of mutual lending such as that mentioned and, naturally, the specific collaborations for agricultural tasks or care of the herds. They thus explained the *minka* as that activity in which common lending made it possible to carry out a work of communal benefit, such as a warehouse, path or bridge. However, the nominal variations since the 16th century to the present leave open various possibilities, above all regarding distinguishing the *minka* from the *mitta*, which was the collaboration of energy in turns, fundamentally destined to the production of goods that could be redistributed among members of the group. Certainly, there was also redistribution at different levels of power, which grouped together greater teams of workers, including the actual organization of Cusco in the times of the Incas. Although traditionally the *ayni*, *minka* and *mitta* have been understood as forms of labor organization, they should always be seen within the context of reciprocity and redistribution.

Reciprocity can also be conceived asymmetrically, even though this consideration depends more on the outside observer, whether a Spaniard of the 16th century or a current day researcher, given that both are situated outside the universe of reciprocity, where the value of a redistributed good is distinct from that which can be attributed to it by a stranger. The asymmetry is taken as a fact given that the good that is "returned" (in reciprocity) or is "received" (in redistribution) does not appear to be equivalent, whether because it consists of an immaterial good (administering the work, directing ritual activities etc.), or whether because the reciprocated or redistributed goods have a high ritual value (clothes, including that given by the *Inca*, *mullu* (*Spondylus* shells used as offerings) or other ritual objects).

On the other hand, the modern examples of *minka* often accentuate the asymmetrical condition. The problem may be that the recipient acquires a preeminent position—possibly from the mere fact of receiving? On administering communal work, the *curaca* is placed in a preeminent position, a situation which he himself recognizes. Nevertheless, it could be argued that this is only a symbolic situation, given that the *curaca* redistributes goods and does not accumulate them for his own benefit. The pure and simple accumulation of goods makes no sense if there is no market.

It is true that this situation of asymmetry is more visible in redistribution than the powers realized, although it should not be placed outside the global characteristics of reciprocity. Redistribution is better understood if we observe examples of the tasks of the *curacas*. The Lupaqa *curacas* already mentioned administered the human energy of the population through *mitta*, or "shifts", realized in distant regions. These were used to obtain products not produced on the shores of Lake Titicaca, where most of the ethnic group lived. Diverse *mittas* allowed agriculture to take place in Moquegua or in Larecaja, to the west and east of the lake respectively. This presumed a *mitta* for sowing, another for harvesting and, perhaps, a third to take the crops to the central warehouses of the ethnic group. Even though the *mitta* and *minka* were described differently in the chronicles, it is not always clear up to what point they may have functioned similarly within the process of redistribution. The *minka* was used for works for the "public good" while the *mitta* was for goods to be stored in the warehouses for subsequent redistribution. This explains why the chroniclers understood that the *ayni*, *minka* and *mitta* were "forms" of collective work.

As the *Tawantinsuyu* grew, so did the process of redistribution covering the wide area across which the empire had grown. The *Inca* established for this purpose kinship relationships with the *curacas*, marrying their young daughters and sisters, or marrying off his own sisters and relatives to the *curacas*. Reciprocal connections were thus developed. The chronicles and other colonial documents have spoken of the "alliances" generated in this way, understood as though they were dynastic accords even though the most visible point of these was that they permitted the *Inca* to access certain types of labor which he could then deploy with greater reliability and outside of the traditional, fixed periods of the *mitta*. However, this is a subject that requires greater research.

The existence of property among the Incas has been severely questioned since the times when the classical chroniclers were writing. On the one hand, its existence along the lines of that known in Europe was simply affirmed, even though this claim was qualified with the specification that property was restricted by the civil or religious authorities, while the people's goods, especially land and livestock, were common. These types of claims varied over time in the historiography of the Incas, allowing the elaboration of collective theories to explain the Inca economy and organization. The chronicles thus spoke generically of the lands of the *Inca*, of the Sun and the people, and of the communitarian administration and distribution, albeit with the participation of the authorities. If today it is feasible to discuss this classically known division, it is also necessary to remember that in the initial moments of the Spanish invasion, there was an unquestioned justification in the *conquistadors'* need to indicate which goods could be adjudicated, without any legal objection, directly to the Spanish crown, even when the purpose was to grant them as "favors" to be distributed among the *conquistadores* or the Church. In the earliest moments of the Spanish period, the lands of the *Inca* and of the Sun were understood as property of the religious bureaucracy and were destined for its use.

The Spanish authors and functionaries who lived in Peru in the 16th century left testimony to the inexistence of property among the people. For example, in 1566, Gregorio González de Cuenca elaborated the "ordinances of the Indians" after a varied decade of life as a Spanish functionary in the Andes. In these, he wrote that the *curacas* sold common land belonging to the population as though it was their own, acknowledging that it belonged to the "community". In this manner, Cuenca stated that the *curacas* did not own land because of their position, but administered the territories of the population they governed. This can be associated with the function of the *curacas*, mentioned in the chronicles, to organize labor on the land for the people's subsistence. On the other hand, the chronicles also indicate that the Incas received lands from each of the ethnic groups incorporated into their dominion. Some authors gather specific local information, such as occurred with Cristóbal de Castro and Diego Ortega Morejón in the Chincha valley, situated on the central coast of Peru; in their celebrated *Description of the Chincha Valley*, they stated that distinct and specifically marked terrains were given to each *Inca*. Each *Inca* thus received his new lands and the text allows us a glimpse of what remained afterwards in the hands of the *panaqa* or kinship group of the *Inca*. We can conclude that the Andean authorities administered and generally established certain lands, given that they constructed terraces for agriculture, and irrigation canals to make these wastelands productive. From what we can tell, the production of these terrains was destined for redistribution, being stored in the *qollqas* or warehouses administered by the different levels of authority, *curaca* or *Inca*.

The chroniclers also indicate that the Incas used the lands of the valleys neighboring Cusco, which were assigned for the use and maintenance of the *panaqa* or kinship groups of the Incas of Cusco, each of which was headed by an *Inca*. This happened specifically with the valley of Yucay, traditionally considered the sacred valley of the Incas. For the cultivation of these lands principally dedicated to the sowing of corn, the Incas used an important number of *yanakuna*, people dedicated to production on behalf of the authorities, who came from distant lands. Colonial documents tell us that the people of Yucay had largely originated from the region of Cañar, in present-day Ecuador, even though other documents from the same era indicate that the Chupaychu, of the Huánuco region in the central mountains of Peru, used to give "400 Indans to sow fields in Cusco in order for the people to eat and make their place". These were given "continuously"; in other words, this number of workers existed on a permanent basis in the aforementioned area. It can be generally stated that the production of the "*Inca's* lands" was dedicated to filling the warehouses of the Cusco administration, whose purpose was to feed those who contributed their human energy to the authorities, as well as maintaining the administration and serving as a reserve. All this leaves the impression that, in Andean terms, the important thing was not so much control over the earth but rather the capacity to administer the labor that made it productive.

In the same way, the chronicles signal the existence of lands of the Sun, the most important "official" divinity of the Incas. In a similar manner to the lands of the *Inca*, those of the Sun were dedicated to the provision of the temples and the people who worked the land, defined along ethnic lines, and the surplus production was included, as in the case of the *Inca's* lands, for redistribution.

Agrarian measurements were also referenced by the chroniclers. They stated that a *tupu* allowed for the provision of one adult and this corresponded to the man; the woman received half a *tupu* when part of a couple. The chroniclers defined a *tupu* as a quantity of products and tell us that its meaning is "measure" or "measurement". It is, at the same time, a unit of volume, given that there is a *tupu* of *chicha* (the word in Runasimi for maize liqueur is *açua*) and also of water. The term also has other related meanings, such as the definition of a distance between two points. But the chroniclers assumed that the population was able to provide for itself in a single place, their residence, and for that reason a *tupu* is generally defined as a plot of land. It can be appreciated, therefore, that the people were expected to move to sometimes distant regions to fulfill diverse *mitas*, organized by their ethnic group. During the *Tawantinsuyu* the *mita* system as well as that of redistribution spread across the region.

It is possible that the *tupu* can also be understood as the quantity of land that one person could cultivate, with 1.5 *tupus* being the amount assigned to one family unit. Nevertheless, the actual area of a *tupu* varied according to the nature and location of the terrain and the crops grown on it. We know that there were distinctions drawn between *tupus* located on terraces and away from them, in the valleys and highlands, as well as those dedicated to growing maize or potatoes, for example. *Tupu* is thus a multiple term.

The chroniclers also tend to state that there were annual distributions of communal lands, although this does not appear to be precisely true and could in reality be the assigning of people to work specific plots of common land dedicated to redistribution. This division of labor can also be explained in the form of a migration or recognition of established reciprocal relations, given that through its administration the *curaca* confirmed the obligations established within the group.

The *papacancha* has been mentioned as an agrarian measurement specifically for the cultivation of potatoes employed in the Cusco region in the 16th century. It was defined as "20 yards wide and 20 long and was only used in cold lands well suited to the cultivation of this tuber". Maria Rostworowski, who has studied this and other Andean measurements, states that the pre-Inca measurements were still used in many areas even during the predominance of the *Tawantinsuyu*, but the *tupu* and *papacancha* were characteristic of the Incas, who spread the former throughout their empire. This does not mean, as we have seen, uniformity in the value of Andean measuring units, as can be appreciated in the colonial documentation and the contemporary ethnographic experience.

Labor

In the Andean economy we can appreciate a general pattern based on the use and administration of labor, but less clearly understood as a tribute to power than as part of a redistributive mechanism. Power in the Andes, whose maximum expression was the Incas of Cusco, used the population's labor in order to produce goods that were difficult to obtain in the immediate vicinity. Considering that production was possible and sufficient thanks to the use of often distant productive areas, power functioned also as the administrator of the population's human energy, which was given in exchange for the distribution of the products thus obtained. A good example is provided by the Lupaqa, inhabitants of the southeastern shores of Lake Titicaca. There it is clearly documented the form in which the *curacas* administered the population's labor under the *mitta* or work groups sent to work shifts on the land in the valleys far from the coast or the southeast of the *altiplano*, in both cases at distances of up to 15 or 20 days walk. In those faraway zones, they obtained resources that were not produced on the *altiplano*, given the particular ecological conditions that existed there at an altitude of 4,000 meters. This happened, for example, with maize, harvestable in the two extremes of the coast and the lowlands located to the east of the Andes. The produce was harvested and stored in the *qollqa* ("warehouses") which the *curacas* administered, distributing it among the population that had contributed to its production. The same thing happened with other resources. In all cases the population provided *mittani* (people fulfilling a *mitta* by turn) and *mitmaqkuna* (people staying a long time in a place of production). This example can be multiplied, with variations, as we will see later.

With the advent of the *Tawantinsuyu*, this system was taken to new levels, as the Incas organized the production of resources from specific zones, ordering for this purpose *mittani* from different ethnic groups. We find a good example of this in a document written in 1556 relating to litigation over land. It mentions that Inca Huayna Cápac, who the chronicles place shortly before the Spanish invasion, distributed the valley of Cochabamba, dividing it into *suyu* or sectors, among numerous ethnic groups, all of which hailed from the *alitplano* of Titicaca and Charcas. Different *mittani* visited the valley at the times of sowing and harvesting, staying in groups of *mitmaqkuna* charged with looking after the seeds. The *Inca* built nearly 2,000 *qollqa* or warehouses in order to store the maize, produced in abundance given that that valley is particularly apt for this crop.

This same issue can be appreciated in an oral tradition which I encountered in the valley of the Colca River, in Arequipa, in the southern mountains of Peru, where the lower part of the valley, known as Cabanaconde, was apparently colonized by the *Inca* Mayta Cápac, one of the first rulers in the genealogical list of Cusco conserved in the chronicles. The contemporary oral version states that when this *Inca* arrived in the zone he observed the goodness of this valley for the cultivation of maize and he made an "army" come from Cusco, which sowed extensive areas with the crop, first constructing irrigation channels and terraces for its cultivation. The *Inca* ordered that no person touch the land in his absence. Seven years later he returned with another "army" of cultivators and harvested the maize, which had developed in the region with seven varieties of distinct colors. The tradition thus attributes to the *Inca* the origin of the maize of Cabanaconde which, up until the present day, is a rival for the most prestigious maize in Peru. It can be appreciated in this case that, as in Cochabamba, the "armies" that the *Inca* mobilized were, in reality, *mittani* dedicated to production.

Agriculture

The history of agriculture in the Andes is lengthy, and it can be stated that there were already multiple examples of its use 1,000 years before Christ. A long time before the Incas, the Andean population had not just domesticated many plants, including the potato in its hundreds of varieties, and maize, but it had also, probably from the times of Tiawanaku, organized cultivation into appropriate ecological zones, in the search for a complementarity that would provide notable efficiency. It maintained at the same time the systematic collection of natural and selected agricultural products, domesticating them and acclimatizing them to diverse conditions. Just by doing this, they managed to notably widen the variety of produce that they obtained, making viable both the semi-arid lands of the coast as well as the inter-Andean valleys, the hillsides and the highlands of the *puna*.

At the beginning of this book, we looked at the general outlines of the Andean environment. It is interesting now to further explore how the Incas, and their ancestors, achieved sufficient control over production, especially agrarian, which allowed the population to achieve a surplus which made possible a comfortable subsistence and the creation of reserves in order to survive droughts and agricultural crises. For this reason, the forms of land use, whose development was significant in the organization of Andean life, are important.

The calculations regarding the size of the Andean population prior to the Spanish invasion are still incipient and, in any case, relate fundamentally to the time of the Incas, 100 years before the arrival of Francisco Pizarro and his band of conquerors. But amid the calculations already carried out, we can accept that, at the very least, the population of the *Tawantinsuyu* could have reached 15 million people.

John V. Murra has developed a hypothesis defined as the "vertical control of a maximum of ecological levels in Andean societies". From this, we can deduce that the Andean population developed, from a long time before the Incas, a system that allowed them to achieve the complementarity necessary to obtain resources only available in specific ecological zones of the Andes, given the unusual configuration of the terrain. One of the suppositions of the ideas of Murra is found in a proposal of Carl Troll, many years earlier, which explains that in the Andes each additional 200 meters of altitude above 2,500m above sea level, and each degree south of the equator implies a change of import ecological variations. Murra highlighted that the Andean ethnic groups controlled distinct ecologies within a notion of territory that obliged the controlled dispersal of the population. For this reason, the people of the southern mountains needed to use lands as much in the coastal valleys as well as those located in the lower areas of the eastern *altiplano* between Peru and Bolivia. Some of the evidence for this theory, about which the debate continues, has been previously mentioned and it can be appreciated that there exist variations according to the region where distinct examples of this theory functioned. Murra initially highlighted five cases, among which the most important were the Lupaqa, and the Chupaychu of Huánuco, in the southern sierra of Peru. In the former case, the basic characteristics were shaped by the great distances separating the nuclear sphere, the banks of Titicaca, from the "colonies" producing maize, chilies, cotton and other products. In this case, shared with variations with other Aymara-speaking ethnic groups of the *altiplano*, the maximum distance between the nucleus and the "colonies" could be from 15 to 20 days walk, with the journey of the camelids used for transport divided into suitable daily marches. We are dealing here with densely populated societies, some of which could reach 100,000 inhabitants. In the second case, that of the Chupaychu, the distances were considerably less (one to five days) and the "colonized" zones were found both in the Andean region as well as towards the rainforest east of the Andes. The population was smaller, with groups of between 15,000 and 18,000 inhabitants. In both these cases, we are dealing with groups whose nuclear range was found in the high Andean zone, from where they always controlled areas of *puna*, up to 4,000 meters above sea level.

A third case proposed by Murra refers to smaller ethnic groups from the central coast, who used spheres of influence or productive "colonies" in the mountains, dedicated above all to the acquisition of coca, chilies and other products not available on the coast, strictly defined. This type of group, as well as others on the southern coast, for example Atico and Caravelí, was found with populations that managed to control areas of *puna* for the grazing of camelids, and who also undertook lengthy journeys towards the north, along the length of the coast and possibly by sea, in order to obtain *mullu* (*Spondylus*, shells used as offerings), which could only be found in warm waters, to the north of the Santa Elena Peninsula in present-day Ecuador.

A fourth case considered by Murra is that of the "great coastal kingdoms", which were densely populated and where irrigation was highly developed, as in Chimor, for example. The problem here is that we lack the rich documentation existing for the three previous cases. Nevertheless, the archaeological record, as well as ethnology, allows an appreciation even in our times of their contacts with the mountains. Finally, the fifth case offered by Murra relates to small groups based in the lowlands to the east of the Andes, in the Bolivian *yungas*, and where apparently there was no "vertical control" with peripheral colonies, but other forms of ecological complementarity, with reduced reach.

Murra's proposal has started a wide debate, opening the discussion about a variety of forms of control of the earth in general, as well as the complementarity of the resources available in the Andes. It has also called attention specifically to the social organization that this system makes necessary, given that it does not solely deal with control of distinct ecologies by an ethnic group, but rather spans the organization of its redistribution among the people who comprise it, adding that the workers in the colony, especially the *mittani*, reserved their reciprocal and redistributive rights during their absence from the nuclear base.

This system of pluri-ecological control allowed for the maximum exploitation of Andean ecological conditions. As we have seen, during the *Tawantinsuyu* the administration of the workforce, which had existed prior to the Incas, was taken to a new scale and with multi-ethnic participation. It is very possible that this land use regime, sustained over great seasonal concentrations of *mittani*, might have functioned in other parts of the Andean area (and not just in the previously referenced examples in Cochabamba and the Colca Valley). Both the chronicles and the colonial documentation have provided abundant information regarding the numerous colonies of *mitmaqkuna* (populations transplanted like permanent colonies) which the *Tawantinsuyu* kept functioning in very diverse Andean zones. The chronicles insisted that these *mitmaqkuna* included among their functions the realization of agricultural labor, and they formed a fundamental part of the mechanisms of political and economic power of the Incas of Cusco.

A vast and impassioned range of discussions has arisen from the study of the coastal economy, where the great human groups of the northern coast (Chimor, for example) developed a flourishing economy based on irrigation prior to and then in coexistence with the *Tawantinsuyu*. Defeated by the Incas and incorporated into the *Tawantinsuyu*, their organization appears to have integrated with the general principals of the Incas. However, there has been a controversy for several years now about whether the coast in general, as well as the Andean zone of present-day Ecuador, functioned within a market economy regime. The most salient examples could be that of the valley of Chincha, on the central Peruvian coast, and the well-known case of the Ecuadorian *mindalaes*, categorized as merchants. In the former case, authors of the 16th century and administrative documents of the era mentioned colonies of these "merchants" who were principally dedicated to the trade of *mullu* (*Spondylus*), which were used for ritual purposes. As this was only available on the northern coast of the Santa Elena Peninsual, in current-day Ecuador (*Spondylus* lives in warm waters and can only be found further south when marine currents, such as that caused by el Niño, for example, extend down the coast in extraordinary conditions), the men of Chincha had to travel to those regions to obtain it, and they must have organized, in consequence, an extensive market in the central zone of the coast. Nevertheless, populations located on the coast immediately south of Chincha sent their people to Santa Elena to get *mullu* for their offerings. This places in question Chincha's status as a great market of *mullu*.

In the case of the *mindalaes*, it has been stated, based on the chronicles, that they were merchants; but we have not obtained verifiable evidence, making it possible that they were travellers charged with making exchanges, which did not necessarily need to be governed by the rules of the market. It should be added that the market has been assumed as much by the Spaniards of the 16th century as by modern authors, but that the evidence of the 16th century is tinted with European stereotypes, with similar preconceptions around the figure of the *Inca* (understood as a European king) or that of religion, organized as a central and unitary church.

Agricultural Technology

Andean man managed to improve soil conditions for agriculture in many ways. The most known are the construction of *andenes* or artificial agricultural terraces for sowing different products even though they are often associated with the cultivation of maize. The *andenes* were certainly used since long before the Incas but research indicates that during the 100 years of Inca supremacy there was an enormous investment in their construction. Without going into prolix explanations, it is sufficient to note that Andean myths present one of the special attributes of the Inca as the ability to make stones move on their own and to order them into *pirqa* or walls, or in other words, the forms of various constructions including, of course, terraces.

71

Equally, a short time after the Spanish invasion, when inspections of or visits to the Andean populations were carried out, the Spaniards asked systematically about any "tribute" given to the *Inca*. In some places, they gained particularly precise information, thanks to the use of quipus (*khipu*), the long cords made with knotted wool of different colors, where accounting information was registered.

In Huánuco, the Chupaychu *curacas* told the Spanish visitors in 1549—just 16 years after the events of Cajamarca—that they placed at the disposition of the *Inca* in Cusco 400 men and their women *to build walls on a continuous basis*. This number was important if we appreciate that it dealt with adults and that the Chupaychu ethnic group numbered between 15,000 and 18,000 members, or roughly 3,000 to 3,500 family units and, in consequence, nearly one seventh of the entire number of heads-of-family were ordered to provide their human energy specifically for these constructions during the *Tawantinsuyu*. If this proportion remained constant across the extensive range of the land of the Incas, the quantity of people dedicated to the construction of buildings, paths, irrigation canals, terraces and warehouses, would have been very significant. All this explains in part why, even in current oral tradition, as in the myths of the 16th century, the *Inca* is said to have had the power to make stones move on their own and to order themselves into walls.

The terraces served many purposes, but were principally for making the land of the steep Andean slopes suitable for agriculture. At the same time, they permitted a better use of water (rainwater as well as irrigation) recycling it through the canals that connected the different levels of terraces, thus avoiding the erosion of the soil. It is very possible that there may have been terraces solely for the purpose of avoiding erosion. They also existed for other specific uses, such as washing the mineral salt (see photo 1).

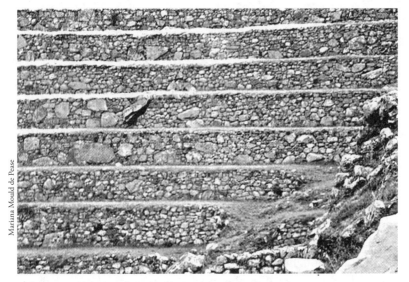

Mariana Mould de Pease

Photo N° 1. Terraces at Machu Picchu

Other forms of land use can also be added; firstly, the ridges or mounds existing in the *puna* around Lake Titicaca. These artificial humps in the earth, creating elevated, cultivable areas above the natural surface of the terrain, allowed for better drainage in zones where the soil is relatively impermeable and subject to frequent flooding. They make possible a better use of water, avoiding its rapid depletion. This is also important because conservation of water is fundamental in the *altiplano*. In some parts of the region, the greater frequency of these ridges coincides with a decrease in the number of terraces. Although the terraces are very ancient, it is noticeable that they continued functioning during the times of the Incas of Cusco.

Similar systems have been used in other parts of the Americas, making wetlands productive (for example, the famous *chinampas* of the Valley of Mexico) and constructions of the same type are found in the seasonally-flooded tropical plains of Colombia, as well as in the Moxos of Bolivia. It is possible, however, that the greatest area of these mounds is that in the lands abutting Lake Titicaca.

Secondly, we should mention another system of use and improvement of the soil that was used, including up to the present day, in the same highlands neighboring Titicaca. This is the so-called *qocha*, or pool, consisting of conical holes in which rainwater was deposited and stored, allowing sufficient reserves to be used for agriculture, including within the actual *qocha*. Naturally, this water could be moved around, from one *qocha* to another, as well as to the surrounding land by a series of canals. The ethnographic information adds that the *qochas* help prevent the *puna* freezing over given that the water absorbs heat during the day, and then releases it at night.

They are thought to be pre-Hispanic constructions, very possibly from before the Incas. If so, they were also employed during the Inca period. The absence of references to the *qochas* in the chronicles and other documents of the 16th century should not surprise us, given that they are located at some distance from the most heavily-used roads, and that what was produced in them did not make its way to the Spanish market, being used instead for daily subsistence. Although there has been little archaeological research into them, some appear to be associated with Inca constructions. Even today they are fundamentally used for the cultivation of different types of potatoes.

The chroniclers of the 16th century provided us with the first information known to Europeans regarding these agricultural techniques or, better stated, of exploitation of the soil. It is true that they did not know all the previously mentioned techniques, but they did insist that they constituted important demonstrations of agricultural development. Attention was also drawn, therefore, to the forms in which the residents of the coast cultivated crops in different zones, beyond the strict limits of the coastal valleys. The use of pits in the ground was one notable technique, as also were excavations in sandy zones to exploit subterranean water bodies. Contemporary studies regarding this pit agriculture have allowed us to prove the continuity of its use as well as its significance in hot zones and deserts such as those existing to the south of Lima, in the department of Ica.

Recent research has also reevaluated the agricultural techniques in the coastal hills. Prior to the Incas, these were used along with other techniques of agricultural exploitation of those times. They involved areas which receive a significant amount of precipitation at certain times of year, allowing sowing of crops, including with the construction of internal irrigation channels. Genuine oases in the desert, they can without doubt be included among the techniques developed in the Andes to make the earth productive.

There is an abundant bibliography about irrigation in the Andes. It covers those societies which developed great irrigation systems on the northern coast of present day Peru (Moche and Chimor) as well as the construction of canals realized in other coastal regions, among which the springs (*puquios*) of underground water used in Nasca stand out. The canals of the intermediate and higher levels of the Andes have also been studied. Although this theme has a very long history, there is much evidence of the intensification of the construction of canals during the time of the Incas, much of it related to the mass construction of terraces. The chronicles tell us of the Incas' task of constructing these canals and reservoirs. Even though the research of recent years has opened up this theme significantly, there remains much to be studied in the field of Andean hydraulic engineering. The relationship between irrigation and power exercised on a grand scale (as occurred in the Andes during the period of the Wari predominance and the reign of Chimor on the northern coast) has been frequently mentioned. But without doubt the expansion of the area under irrigation formed part of the political economy of the Incas. Many researchers have made a special point of the way in which the hydraulic technology of the northern coast developed more than that of other political organizations in the mountains, until the conquest of Chimor and the northern Andes by the Incas allowed these patterns of irrigation to become generalized.

Andean man did not use animal energy for agriculture. For this purpose, his tools were basically manual and can be considered generalized across the entire Andean region. There is no evidence that these basic tools were perfected during Inca times; in any case, it is thought that their use spread into areas where it had not existed previously. The contemporary use of these tools is still visible, and they have not been replaced in many parts of the Andes after four centuries of European presence. This also demonstrates the current usefulness of Andean technology, extended into many other activities and not just limited to the construction of tools. The *chaquitajlla* or foot-plough has not been improved upon for use on the steep Andean slopes, nor in the tight spaces used for agriculture, especially in the terraces that remain in use.

Llama or alpaca manure was generally used for fertilizer. The herds of camelids were used for this on arable land, through complicated rotation processes which are still being studied today. On the coast, guano was also used, from the littoral islands as well as that deposited by birds during millennia on the coast itself. This was collected by the population for its use not just on the coast but also in the highlands, where it was transported on the backs of llamas. Fish-heads were also used for fertilizer on the coast, and were buried with the seeds.

Livestock

Livestock has had an enormous significance in the economic organization of the Andean region and that was certainly the case during the times of the Incas. The camelid species in the Andes are the llama (*Lama glama*), alpaca (*Lama pacos*), vicuna (*Lama vicugna*) and guanaco (*Lama guanicoe*). In general terms, the first two are the largest, with the llama reaching around three feet in height [at the withers] and approximately 250 pounds in weight, with the alpaca of lesser stature and weight. The guanaco is probably the most widely spread, in geographical terms, as it has been found from areas just south of the Equator to Tierra del Fuego.

The llama has been primarily used as a beast of burden, although as clearly secondary functions it also provides meat and wool. The meat from elderly animals was used to make *charki* (meat dried in the Sun) which helped conserve it for later consumption. Alpaca meat was the most used for human consumption. Alpaca wool was also used for weaving and there were various natural colors. The vicuna and guanaco were wild; some information speaks of *chaku*, the "hunting" of vicunas, with the discovery of archaeological remains including structures that may well have served to enclose vicunas and shear them, for their wool was highly esteemed, especially for the clothes of the *Inca*, as the chronicles repeatedly note.

These camelids were initially hunted. Eight thousand years ago the hunting of guanacos was a fundamental part of the economy of the nomadic inhabitants of the highlands of the central Andes, especially in the *altiplano* of central Peru, around Junín and Huánuco, and the areas neighboring Lake Titicaca. In the northern Andes, where the altitude decreases markedly and the *puna* disappears, camelids are rare or nonexistent, although there is data that mentions the introduction of livestock in the region conquered by the Incas. The dates of domestication are still uncertain but archeologists claim there is evidence for this in the mountains of Chavín 1,000 years before Christ. This domestication must be especially linked to weaving and its spread, with pasture turning into an activity of the greatest importance in the highlands, given that the natural habitat of the camelids was *puna*. It was there that the greatest concentration of these animals was found.

In the times of the Incas, pasture and the use of livestock resources was without doubt one of the most important sectors of the Andean economy. We have already seen that the Incas occupied the *altiplano* around Lake Titicaca during the first moments of their expansion, and we also can appreciate that this was one of the most important zones for camelids. The ethnic groups who lived there based a good part of their economy on livestock. For example, it is unthinkable that the Lupaqa could have transported the products obtained from their distant colonies on the Pacific coast or in the lower parts of *altiplano* in modern day Peru and Bolivia without great herds of llamas. On the other hand, we can also observe that the chronicles relate that the journeys of the *Inca*, both in times of peace and war, were accompanied by the ritual distribution of clothing made from wool principally from alpacas of the *altiplano*. The chronicles state that the Incas' state storehouses, built across the length and breadth of the *Tawantinsuyu*, were full of woolen cloth used by the *Inca* for redistribution. The same happened with the storehouses of the ethnic groups, administered by the *curacas*. It can therefore be said that during the time of the Incas the production and consequent use of woolen cloth spread and became generalized, and we can even consider that, with it being one of the principal vehicles of redistribution, woolen clothing effectively contributed to the financing of the expansion of the *Tawantinsuyu*.

The herds were administered both by the *Tawantinsuyu* and by the ethnic groups. According to the ample data existing regarding the ethnic groups of the Titicaca region, before and after the Incas, we can appreciate the enormous importance of camelids in daily life. But what is also notable is the sheer number of animals available to the population, the *curacas* and the *Inka*. The data about the last camelids registered in the hands of the Andean authorities may have been altered, given that almost as soon as the Spanish invasion took place the herds of the *Inca* were adjudicated as either belonging to the Crown or to be shared among the Spaniards. As a result, the population rapidly took to hiding these animals, either placing them in remote areas or incorporating them into communal or personal herds. This last point is interesting given that even in the times of the Viceroy Francisco de Toledo (1572) there were "rich Indians" registered in the census realized during the visit to Chucuito; their wealth consisted of the ownership of camelids. Despite the insistence of the chronicles in qualifying the *Tawantinsuyu* as general "owner" of goods, it can be stated that this is not entirely correct as a considerable quantity of the herds remained in the hands of the population at the time of the Spanish invasion.

The herds "of the *Inca*" and "of the Sun" appear to have been primarily destined for redistribution, as well as more specific purposes related to the manufacturing of cloth for the elite and those associated with religious activities. The population delivered quantities of labor towards the care and maintenance of these herds, the cloth and other tasks. All this constituted part of the *mitta* of the Andes as it was classically understood, and this is how it appears in the documentation. It is very possible that in the same way that occurred with the sowing, *mitmaqkuna* and even *yana* were assigned to fulfill the ongoing functions dictated by the care of the herds.

The chroniclers leave us testimony regarding the volume of the herds. Inca Garcilaso de la Vega even stated: "The Indians used to say that when the Spaniards arrived on that land, they did not have anywhere to graze their livestock." Pedro Cieza de León had noted similar points previously, adding that there were a great number of guanacos and vicunas. Cieza also explained, similarly to other authors, that during the Spanish era the numbers of both the domesticated herds and wild animals had greatly diminished. Although Cieza stated that the civil wars that took place among the Spaniards in the 1540s had caused the drastic decline in the number of camelids, it should also be pointed out that at the same time, and as a consequence of various causes including the importation of European animals, new epidemics began which would decimate the Andean livestock population in the following decades.

The chroniclers talked repeatedly of the *chaku* or Andean chaco, as those grand occasions of mass hunting, which included not just the rounding up of dispersed herds but also of wild animals. Some chroniclers indicated that the *chaku* could include pumas, bears, deer (*taruka*), etc., referring to a generalized activity which the chroniclers themselves identified as the excursions of Spanish hunting parties. The *Inca* and, naturally, the ethnic lords took part in the *chaku*, as well as the population which participated as a form of *mitta*. There are testimonies from the 16th century to this effect as well as the actual chronicles, which include this activity among the "tributes" that were delivered to the *Tawantinsuyu* of the Incas. It is notable that the *chaku* was a term that denoted various tasks, and we need to distinguish between those used to gather domesticated herds and those that involved the herding together of wild animals. Grouping together herding and indiscriminate hunting as a single activity does not appear possible.

Inca Garcilaso de la Vega described the *chaku* in his *Royal Commentaries of the Incas* thus:

> [...] at a certain time of the year, after the breeding season, the *Inca* headed for the province which suited his whim and which the conditions of peace or war permitted. He ordered 20,000 or 30,000 Indians, or thereabouts, to head out, who were needed to partition off the area of land. The Indians were divided into two parts; one headed to the left and the other to the right, in a line, making a great circle of 20 or 30 leagues of land, more or less, according to the district which they needed to enclose. They took the rivers, streams and tributaries that were indicated by boundaries or the chiefs of the land they were

hunting that year, and did not enter the district that was meant to be hunted the following year. They moved along shouting and beating at however many animals they had in front of them, and they already knew where they had to go and halt and gather the two arms of the people in order to embrace the circle that they had made and corral the livestock that they had gathered. And they also knew where they had to go and halt the beating, which was a clean land with mountains, crags and rocks, because it did not hinder the hunting. Once there, they closed the hunt in, with three or four walls of Indians, until they were able to take the animals with their hands.

With the hunting they captured lions and bears and many foxes, cats called *ozcollo*, of which there are two or three species, genets and other similar creatures, which cause harm in the hunt. They killed all these afterwards in order to clean the land of that bad rabble. Of tigers, we make no mention because there are none in the mountains of the Andes but in the forest. The number of deer, roebuck and buck, and larger animals called vicuna, which are slim and with very fine wool, was very great. Many times, and according to the lands, some of which were more hunted on than others, there were 20,000, 30,000 and 40,000 head, a beautiful thing to see and of much joy. This was then. Now, say those present, the number of guanacos and vicunas which have escaped the destruction and waste of the arquebuses, is barely found, in the places where they [the Spaniards] have not been able to reach.

The author emphasizes the *chaku* as an activity of power, translating the terms without fail for the reader: In the Andes, there are no lions, but rather pumas, and there are no deer, but rather *taruka*, a similar but evidently distinct species. Nevertheless, he does provida proof of the decline of these species based on the indiscriminate hunting of the Spanish times.

Metallurgy

Andean metallurgy is ancient. Around the era of Chavín predominance (1000 B.C.) there were already clear signs of its advanced artistic and technological development. The chroniclers of the 16th century rapidly popularized the account that the Incas had developed important jewelry, and the proof of this was the many pieces of gold and silver mentioned from the very first moments of the Spaniards' appearance on the region's coasts. For example, the account attributed to Juan de Sámano and Francisco de Xerez (the former was secretary to Carlos V and the latter was effectively a chronicler and not the most certain author of the relevant account) mention a raft found on the coast of Tumbes, in which abundant precious metal objects were discovered. One well-known "French account" of the conquest of Peru likewise states that life-sized llamas made of gold were also found. Other important accounts appear when the chroniclers relate the events of Cajamarca, after the capture of the *Inca* Atahualpa, and describe the many pieces of gold and silver which were brought there from very distant parts of the *Tawantinsuyu* in order to meet the "ransom" agreed between the *Inca* and Francisco Pizarro. On that occasion, many pieces were accounted for, not just in the descriptions of the chroniclers but also in the notarial documents that were used for the accounts of the melted metals, regarding which a tax had to be paid to the Spanish king.

The accounts of the riches of gold and silver found in the extensive territories of the Inca dominion filled the pages of the chronicles and the descriptions of Peru that were published at that time in Europe, giving birth to an authentic legend of lost gold. Later on, the chroniclers related extraordinary things, speaking, for example, of the famous "garden of gold" of Coricancha, dedicated to the Sun and the most important temple of Cusco. There, according to Inca Garcilaso de la Vega in his *Royal Commentaries of the Incas*, were represented all the important plants and animals that existed in the land of the Incas. The fame of this gold rapidly spread among the Spaniards, not just in the Americas but also in Spain, and the 16th century is known in Peru for the relentless searches for treasure on the one hand, while on the other expeditions were organized to discover legendary cities of gold based on old European fables and which always seemed to be just beyond the last known Spanish settlement.

The gold was obtained in the Andes in fluvial washes and also in mines. The very first chroniclers detailed the way the mines worked. For example, Pedro Sancho wrote in 1534:

> The mines are in the shaft, in a river, at around half its depth, made in the manner of caves through whose mouth they enter to dig the earth and they dig it with stag horns and they carry it out with certain stitched leathers in the form of sacks or of wineskins made from sheepskins. The way in which they wash it is that they take it out of the river a [there is a gap in Sancho's text here] of water and on the bank they have placed very smooth slabs onto which they throw the earth and they throw onto this water through a pipe with [another gap], which falls on top of it and the water carries away the soil bit by bit, and what is left on the slabs is gold and in this way they collect it. The mines go deep into the earth, around 10 fathoms, and others 20. They have no light nor do they have enough width other than for a bent-over person to enter.

The chronicler was describing some mines in Colloa, subsequently known by the name of Porco, south of the present-day city of La Paz.

The other most used metals in the Andes (silver, copper, tin, etc.) were obtained by mining, by tunneling as well as by the method described above, and from surface reserves, of which there are examples in the south-eastern slopes of the Andes. Bronze had been known from ancient times, although it was widely spread by the Incas. After they conquered the Chimor region, in the northern coast of Peru, they particularly spread the use of bronze made from copper and tin, thus replacing arsenical bronze.

The chroniclers, especially P. Miguel Cabello Balboa, gathered information about the Inca conquest of Chimor, and spoke of an enormous booty brought to Cusco by the *Inca* Pachacuti approximately 70 years before the Spanish invasion. A considerable part of this booty had consisted in pieces of gold and silver. Cabello Balboa writes that the Incas arrived in the valley "of the Chimo where incredible, copious riches of gold and silver were found". The conquest had been carried out by Tupa Inca Yupanqui, whom the chroniclers described as the son of Pachacuti, and Cabello Balboa added: "Of the gold and silver that Topa Ynga brought on this voyage, he ordered Yngayupangui (the name that Cabello gives to Pachacuti) to make a statue of the Sun and of Ticciviracocha and of Mama Ocllo Ynga illo, and he also made the belt of gold that is in Curicancha, and he left another great property in the exchequer or public deposit with which he made Cusco so rich just like our Spaniards discovered it afterwards." The Inca conquest of Chimor must be associated with the spread of specific *mitmaqkuna* across numerous areas in the Andes, namely smiths hailing from that region. They also appear registered as "silversmiths" in the documentation of the 16th century.

The ethnic groups submitted by the *Tawantinsuyu* of the Incas provided manual labor for the mines in a similar way to multiple other state activities. Thus, the Chupchayu, of the Huánuco region, stated in 1549 that: "...of every 100 Indians, they threw [into the gold mines] three Indian men and three Indian women and kept them there for the whole year and that the gold which they brought out was taken to Cusco and that each of the four groups gave in this way 60 Indian men and 60 Indian women to bring out silver all year round and they took it from Yaros [another region in Huánuco] and brought it to Cusco."

These metals were melted down in *guayras*, which were a type of small clay oven, whose walls had small holes through which entered the air that fed the fire. For fuel, they used coal or llama dung. After the Spanish invasion, the guayras continued in use, including on a grand scale, as happened in the celebrated city of Potosí, where the Spaniards organized the great silver mine.

The Administration of Production

It is well known that the land of the Incas achieved notable successes in administering production and distribution across the wide space that it occupied. For this purpose, the *Tawantinsuyu* used interesting methods, with the first of these being an extensive network of roads, the *Qhapaq Ñam* or "path of the lord", generally known since the 16th century as the "path of the Inca", although in reality many of its stretches hailed from the Wari era. The chroniclers of the 16th century left many descriptions of these roads, which they frequently compared with those of the Roman empire. For example, Pedro Cieza de León (whose first volume of the *Chronicles of Peru* would be published in Seville in 1553) offers an interesting account that details his personal experience of Inca roads. He states that, at the orders of the Incas, the *curacas* of the coast: "... made a road as wide as 15 feet. And in some parts of it there went a wall larger than [that of] a very strong estate. And all the space of this road was clean, and was beneath lines of trees. And from these trees, in many places, fell branches full of fruits. And in the all the woods, there passed through the trees many types of birds and parrots and other fowl."

Cieza refers specifically to the road on the northern coast of Peru. In the mountains, there was an equivalent route, running longitudinally like that on the coast, and connected with it by a series of transversal roads. Several of the chroniclers highlighted the fact that the mountain road followed the *puna*; in other words, the highest zones, only entering the valleys when it was appropriate.

Photo N° 2. Inca road on the coast (Chala).

Photo N° 3. Inca road in the Andes.

The mountain roads were built with flat stones and there were frequent stairways in order to pass high points, as occurred in the case mentioned in the first chapter, when we cited the pages of P. José de Acosta, in which he related his experience at altitude. There, in Pariacaca (the name of a snowy mountain range and also of an ancient deity of the region) an enormous stone stairway was built, which was travelled over by the Jesuit Acosta, occasioning the disturbance which his text mentions.

Both in the sierra and on the coast, existed many secondary roads which connected many places not on the main route. Proof of the extent of this network of roads can be found in the map, created as a result of the recent research of John Hyslop. The chroniclers of the 16th century emphasized the fact that the paths were already in poor condition a few years prior to the disappearance of the *Tawantinsuyu*. This was above all due to the fact that once the Inca administration had collapsed, the recently-installed colonial regime did not pay sufficient attention to the roads. This situation was naturally evident on the coast, where the sand quickly blew over the roads once the administration of manual labor for their upkeep disappeared.

Tampu or "inns" had been built along the length of these roads, structures which the Spanish of the 16th century referred to as *posadas*. It is possible that they effectively functioned as lodging for travellers but the shape of their various rooms suggests other uses. The first, which is frequently mentioned by the chroniclers, is that of serving as lodging for the *Inca's* armies, as well as the numerous porters and accompaniers who made up his ritual retinue. The chroniclers thus indicate that there were *tampu* specifically for the lodging of the governor of Cusco on his journeys across the territory of the *Tawantinsuyu*. All kinds of provisions were stored there: woolen and cotton clothing as well as food and arms. The information from the chroniclers and the documents of the 16th century describing Andean life, as well as modern archaeology, allow us to see that the *tampu* did not just serve to meet the needs of travellers; they also were integrated into the distributive network of Inca power. It is very possible that when the chronicles mention that the *Inca* distributed clothing and food during his journeys, much of those goods came from the *tampu* along the routes which the *Inca* travelled. The *tampu* were serviced by *mitta* or work in turns, which was needed not just for maintenance but also for the service provided to potential users and for timely distribution of the goods stored in their deposits.

Tampu is a generic term, also used to denote the places where caravans of llamas, transporting resources from regions of production to the places where there was the greatest density of population of a given ethnic group, would pass the night. For this reason, they were placed along the routes which connected the nuclear areas of the different ethnicities with the "colonies" or ecological zones where products were obtained that complemented the resources of the population. On the roads which ascended and descended, the *tampu* were located at different intervals so as to be appropriate for the varying distances the camelids would travel each day. They also had corrals to house the animals.

Like other Andean societies, the Incas built bridges of various forms, some of which are still used today. Those made of ropes from maguey or cat-tail fibers are particularly famous, constructed with three ropes lengthwise, with one placed low for the feet, and the other two higher like handrails. Bridges were also built with two ropes forming the base, with branches placed over them to form a pathway. Others were described thus by Pedro Pizarro, a relative of the leader of the Spanish band, who wrote in 1571 in *Relation of the Discovery and Conquest of the Kingdoms of Peru*:

These Indians used these bridges made from some wide cords, with these cords woven around some sticks in the manner of wickerwork. They made these cords very long, and wider than two hand-spans, and long enough to go from one side of the river to the other with some left over. They also had made some very thick stone bastions in some places, crossed by some very thick beams where the cords were tied, joining them one to the other, and putting some others higher in the manner of a parapet. Afterwards, they threw many thick branches on top, of the width of three or less fingers, and these were bundled together tightly and evenly on top of the cords, placed where one would walk. On top of these branches other long ones were placed, which blocked the sides in the manner of protection, so that no one who paused and looked at the water below could fall. Once made in this manner, and so strong, horses and people could pass very well over them.

The same Pedro Pizarro described another bridge made from rafts, crossing the Desaguadero River, which flows from Lake Titicaca. As can be observed, these bridges required regular reconstruction, given the material from which they were made. This reconstruction and maintenance of the bridges was undertaken by the shift workers or *mittani*.

Storehouses

If the *tampu* were also storehouses built along the length of the roads, the policy of storing resources reached a noted level of development in the Andes, especially during the *Tawantinsuyu* of the Incas. The first chroniclers of the 16th century were already calling attention on the storehouses of food, clothing and other objects that they found in their first journeys through the Andean lands. Leaving testimony of his stay in Cajamarca and the actions of the Spanish that culminated with the capture of the last *Inca*, Atahualpa, Francisco de Xerez wrote in his *True Relation of the Conquest of Peru and the Province of Cusco*

Called New Castille (1534): "In this town of Cajamarca certain houses were found full of clothing tied up in bundles packed to the roofs of the houses. They say that they were stored to supply the army. The Christians took what they wanted and the houses were still so full that what was taken appeared not to have been missed."

Other chroniclers detailed the minutiae of all kinds of objects that were kept in the storehouses but our attention is most drawn to their descriptions of the destination of the food. In 1547, Pedro de Cieza de León saw those in charge of the deposits of Jauja register in their *quipus* everything which was deposited there, as well as everything which had gone missing. This took place in the time of Pedro de la Gasca, President of the Court of Lima and vanquisher of the rebellion of the *encomenderos* led by Gonazalo Pizarro. This same incident was corroborated by Juan Polo de Ondegardo, one of the most zealous observers of the Andes of that period. This information was gathered subsequently; the Jesuit Bernabé Cobo, who wrote around 1653, noted that when the troops of Gasca had passed through Jauja and its valley they had found so much food in the storehouses, that they were able to provision themselves for six months.

The Spaniards noted not just the abundance in the storehouses but also their strategic distribution. Other chroniclers, such as the Andean Felipe Guamán Poma de Ayala, emphasized that each region of the Andes had great collections of storehouses that housed the region's products. When, in the modern era, we have found colonial documents that explain specialized forms of production, for example in the maize-growing valley of Cochabamba, what is striking in them is the construction of thousands of *qollqa* or storehouses where the products are stored. There are many examples of this, and we should stress that the urban nucleuses built by the Incas housed a great number of buildings used as storehouses, as demonstrated in Huánuco Pampa.

Generally the storehouses were built in the highest and driest zones. Their construction, as well as the storage process, formed part of the *mitta* system and the transporting of the goods to the storehouses was also part of the productive process. The storehouses built by the ethnic groups, where production destined for daily consumption was housed, were managed by the ethnic authorities, the *curacas*. But the chroniclers also indicate that there were special people in charge, known as *qollqa kamayuq*, who administered the storehouses built by the central power, where goods were housed to supply the mechanics of redistribution.

The Quipus

Khipus, the famous knotted cords which stored information, were used for administrative accounts in the *Tawantinsuyu*. It is well known that civilization is often identified with writing, and the absence of writing among the Incas has been much discussed, but without considering that until recently writing, as we know it, is one of the symbolic forms of representation used by man. The Andean peoples, John H. Rowe, once wrote, had satisfactory substitutes for writing in the quipus, which in reality are a complex system of registering information.

The quipus were known to the Spaniards of the 16th century, and the chroniclers wrote at length about them. They used the information contained in them (although without learning how they worked) by ordering specialists to "read" the quipus on repeated occasions. Thus, we find descriptions of the "tributes" that were given to Cusco, as well as calculations of the size of the population classified by age and activity. In the same way, when the Andean *curacas* in the 16th century presented various demands or requests claiming to have delivered goods or people to the *conquistadors*, they provided and translated their quipus to the clerks who drafted the corresponding information in Spanish. Once in the early days of the Colony, the Andean quipus replaced books as the method of registering tribute to the Spanish, when the books were destroyed in the contest among the Spaniards for control of the Andes.

The quipu consists of a principal cord, without knots, to which the others, usually of diverse colors, shapes and sizes, are attached, usually by tying. There can also be cords without knots as well as cords which are not attached to the principal cord but to a secondary one. We now understand that the color and perhaps also the form of braiding of the cords indicate the objects to which they refer while the knots express quantities, including the number zero. The quipus known to date vary noticeably in size. There are some very simple ones as well as some examples of more than one thousand cords. Many of the quipus we have today come from archaeological excavations, especially given that at certain moments of the colonization—above all during the campaigns of eradication of Andean "idolatries"—the Spaniards burnt them in great quantities, considering them to be associated with pre-Christian religious practices that they were looking to banish.

In the times of the Incas the quipus were used for purposes of accounting rather than as "writing", although several chroniclers stated that they also contained records of the deeds of the Incas. They were used with precision for the calculations of populations, and for the organization of *mittas* in which members of numerous ethnic groups participated. They were also used to account for what was kept in the storehouses and for production etc. They were also evidently used to account for the quantities of human energy delivered under the regime of reciprocality, not just on a grand scale but also regarding individual family units.

One demonstration of the complexity of data contained in the quipus can be found in the information transcribed by the Spaniards as proof in administrative or judicial proceedings. In one of these, elaborated in Jauja, are detailed for example the quantities of each good delivered by the *curacas* and people of the region to the Spaniards who, commanded by Francisco Pizarro, were passing through the valley for the first time. They added the quantities of people used as porters or auxiliaries of the Spanish group and, finally, they included everything that was either voluntarily given to the Spaniards or stolen by them over a number of years. Surely, this accounting of the goods and services provided to power was related to the Andean tradition of providing human energy and specific goods in return for redistribution, which was then interrupted by the Spanish invasion.

Chapter IV
The Organization of Society

The Dualism

One of the most salient characteristics of Andean social organization is dualism, the roots of which originate in kinship and manifest themselves in the dualist division existing in the ethnic groups in the urban zones of Cusco and in the *Tawantinsuyu* in general. In fact, the chroniclers classified the information they gathered relating to the biographies of the *Incas* in a dual way; the Cusco "dynasties" were *hanan* Cusco *and urin* Cusco. This dualism was also manifest in the organization of the *ayllus* or kinship groups, which appear grouped into *hanan* or *urin* "factions": *alaasa* or *masaa*, *uma* or *urco*, *allauca* or *ichoc* in various parts of the Andes. These terms can be understood as "upper-lower", "right-left", "masculine-feminine", "inner-outer" or even "near-far" and "ahead-behind". When it came to describing Cusco itself, the chroniclers privileged the "upper-lower" relationship, identifying it with the two spheres into which the sacred city is divided, taking into consideration that each of these two halves (*hanan Cusco* and *urin Cusco*) was represented by a "dynasty" of governors. The sources from outside Cusco privileged other terms, such as the case of *alaasa-masaa* in the Aymara-speaking regions, where the *uma-urco* relationship, based directly on proximity or distance to water, also figured, as occurred in the region of Lake Titicaca and its neighboring rivers. *Allauca-ichoc* or "right-left" is the most frequent in parts of the northern Andes.

It is difficult to specify in concrete terms the many functions that this dual organization had in the Andes. The most evident is that this duality shaped reciprocity. This is explained by the fact that *hanan* and *urin curacas* were clearly complementary in the organization of an ethnic half or section. For example, among the Lupaqa of Chucuito, on the banks of Lank Titicaca, the ethnic group was itself divided into two sections or halves "in all the province of Chucuito", each one of which was administered by an equivalent *curaca*; Martín Cari and Martín Cusi were about 30 years old in 1567 when Garci Diez de San Miguel began his official visit to the region on behalf of the viceroyalty. They each belonged to the respective "halves" of the ethnic group and, between the two of them, governed the group. The Spaniards insisted greatly in the 16th century on the existence of a hierarchy that privileged the *hanan curaca*. Thus, from the earliest chronicles regarding the Andean population, there appears a supremacy within the dualist relationship, possibly motivated by the fact that the Europeans of that period were only able to conceive of power individually, as occurred with the *Inca*, although in the same chronicles the notion of *urin* as "before" and *hanan* as "afterwards" appears to be favored when dealing with Inca dynasties.

If the presence of the two "factions" (*hanan-urin, allauca-ichoc,* etc.) is as evident as that of the *curacas* who headed them, and these corresponded to each other as halves, the territorial configuration of these halves is less obvious, as well as archeologically difficult. The chronicles indicated, for example, the division of Cusco as well as the sub-division of its two sections into two other pairs. The same occurs in the archeological evidence gathered in centers such as Huánuco

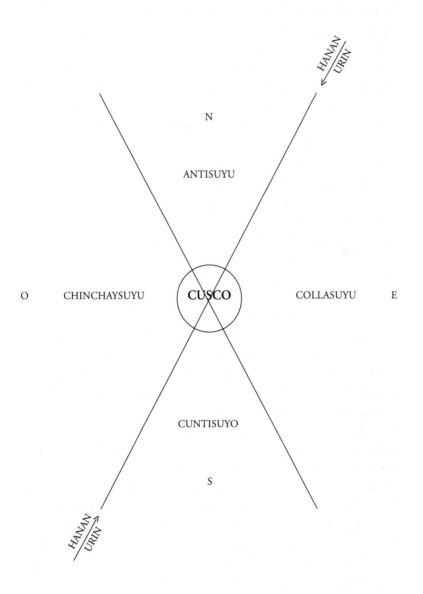

Pampa. Although there are abundant sources regarding this dual organization, physical precision becomes more difficult at smaller scales as, for example, each *cabecera* or town of those described in the Spanish administrative accounts of Chucuito was itself subdivided into new halves. This makes evident a hierarchy, with halves that together constituted an entire ethnic group and subdivisions which can be appreciated in each of the "factions" that constituted it.

Finally, the one thing that remains clear is the complementarity of these halves and the existence of reciprocal obligations among them. In the case of Cusco, the chroniclers were united in noting that the two original halves were themselves subdivided, with four large sectors thus delimited corresponding to the names of Chinchaysuyu, Antisuyu, Collasuyu and Cuntisuyu. The first two formed the *hanan* half, and the last two the *urin* half. Within the *hanan* half, this division was reproduced, and thus Chinchaysuyu was *hanan* in its relation to Antisuyu, which was *urin* in this pairing. The same thing happened in the *urin* half, where Collasuyu was *hanan* in relation to Cuntisuyu. In consequence, Anitisuyu and Cuntisuyu were in turn the respective *urin* sectors of each of the great sections or halves of Cusco.

Dualism was thus an organizing principal in the Andes, functioning at diverse levels even though it is not yet clear the maximum reach that this may have had. *Hanan* and *urin* are opposed and complementary, or *yanantin*, like a pair of hands, and this can be clearly appreciated in the functioning of the halves of the ethnic groups and their respective subdivisions (as we have seen in Cusco). But at the same time, the chroniclers explained that the spatial notion of *suyu* had multiple facets: *Suyu* is each of the four parts of Cusco and the world, but *suyu* is also, for example, the area which each of the various ethnic groups had to cultivate, with their *mittani* working in a large valley such as that of Cochabamba, which as we have previously seen, appeared to have been distributed in the times of the *Inca* Huayna Cápac among different ethnic groups of the *altiplano* who collaborated in a gigantic *mitta* organized by the *Inca*.

The appearance of these "halves" and subdivisions of the world is registered in myths that the chroniclers gathered. A good example is that provided by Juan de Betanzos, who wrote:

> And as the Count Tici Viracocha had already settled this and gone in the manner stated, they say that the two who remained there in the town of Tiaguanaco, that he sent them likewise in order to call and bring out the people in the manner which you had already heard [that is, "from the caves, rivers and sources of the high mountains"], dividing these two in this manner. He sent one to the part and province of Condesuyu which is, being in this Tiaguanaco, with its back to where the sun rises, on the left side ... and he also sent the other to the part and province of Andesuyu, which is on the right-hand side, placed in the stated manner, with its back towards where the sun rises.

In this way, the four *suyu* remain clearly identified: Chinchaysuyu to the west, Antisuyu to the north, Collasuyu to the east and Cuntisuyu to the south.

The hierarchy of the *suyu* was clearly defined, given that if Chinchaysuyu and Collasuyu were *hanan* in their respective halves, the former belonged to the general *hanan* Cusco half, having as a consequence primacy. The order of the *suyu* must then have been: 1) Chinchaysuy, 2) Collasuyu, 3) Antisuyu, 4) Cuntisuyu. Nevertheless, the chronicler Felipe Guamán Poma de Ayala assigned four "lords" to Chinchaysuy and Collasuyu but only two to Antisuyu and Cuntisuyu. This explains that Guamán Poma recognised the primacy of the *hanan* sectors (Chinchaysuy and Collasuyu) over the urin (Antisuyu and Cuntisuyu). At the same time, the chronicler completed the "royal council" conformed by these "lords" with two *Incas*, one from *hanan* Cusco and the other from *urin* Cusco. A clear image of dualism at every level, including that of the *Inca*, is thus formed.

As the chroniclers indicated, Inca Cusco included within each *suyu* a number of *ceques* or imaginary lines that crossed the *huacas* or sacred places that the early chroniclers called temples, regarding which various theories have been proposed to make sense of the social organization of Cusco. The *panaqa* or kinship groups of the Incas and the *ayllus* of Cusco appear to be placed in a hierarchy and related among themselves through marriages of the *Incas*. It is thought that they were ordered into a hierarchy of three groups: Collana, Payán and Cayao, which represented distinct grades of kinship. The Incas who founded the *panaqas* corresponded to the Collana groups; the *panaqas* themselves to the Payán; and the *ayllus* of Cusco to the Cayao *ceques*. This proposal, elaborated by R.T. Zuidema, assumed dualist principles (division into two and four), and a "tri-partition". A creative debate on this subject is still needed.

The Inca

Presented in the chronicles as the "son of the Sun", the *Inca* was interpreted by the Spaniards as a king in the European style, an individual monarch. But local documentation and the chronicles indicate clearly a duality of authority. In the account of Betanzos, Cusco itself was founded by Ayar Manco and Ayar Auca, and there is no specific reason to suppose that the dual organization of Cusco (*hanan* and *urin*) did not require two authorities as was the case with all the ethnic groups mentioned in the documentation. As the Spaniards established the notion of a unique authority, the king, one of the authorities, the *hanan*, was evidently privileged even though in Cusco the *urin* and *hanan* factions were presented as sequential "dynasties", with the *hanan* Incas in power when the Spanish invasion took place.

The chronicles, however, do provide word of an authority understood as a duality, both in Cusco as well as in the *curacazgos* of diverse regions of the Andes, and the accounts of the chronicles often even present two military chiefs in many of the expeditions of the conquest. In the same way, the chronicles place the *Incas* into two sequential dynasties and order the *curacas* into a hierarchy with a principal *curaca* and a "second person". This may be a Spanish judgment, as can be seen with the author Pedro Pizarro, who presented Francisco Pizarro as "captain general" of the group and Diego de Almagro as his "second person", or his lieutenant, in other words. The chronicles also gathered data that allows us to see a conflict, which may well have been ritual, when each *Inca* took power. For this reason, authors such as María Rostworowski de Diez Canseco have proposed the formula of a "co-kingdom" of two Incas as part of the process of selection for the final accession to power.

The *Inca* is presented in the chronicles as a sacred being, who consecrated everything that came into contact with him. He is a mediator between the different planes of the world and, according to some, "the Sun of the earth" in such a way that his power went beyond the mere political domain. This implies that *Inca* is a term whose meaning cannot be reduced to "king", but rather is much broader and more varied.

José María Arguedas noted once that *Inca* was equivalent to "originating model of all being"; in other words an archetype. In Aymara, *enqa* is also a vital and generating beginning or element. As administrator of the greatest redistributive regimes, the *Inca* could be presented in the Andean oral tradition as the originator or giver of maize, as well as other products such as coca, *mullu*, and water, etc. As such, he was the organizer of wide systems of *mitta*, and could also appear as able to make stones order themselves into walls. See the following oral account which I encountered in the 1970s in the Colca River valley (Arequipa):

> *Inkarripa, camachisca, pachamama,* holy earth. For this, we believe up to the present time that *Inkarrí* was apparently like a miraculous god, who, when water was needed, *Inkarrí* would say: 'Let there be water in this place.' And there appeared water. In that very instant, appeared a small eye [*sic*] of water. He wanted to build *chacras*, in other words terraces [and] they built them on their own; the stones turned into walls, they formed terraces on their own.
>
> They say that in Callalli, from the high part, the *Inkarrí* once came down to that region, starting with Callalli. In Callali the *ayllus* greatly respected the *Inca*. Callalli, Sibayo ... and the *Inca* just left them firewood and livestock because it was so high that it was not possible to sow crops. Firewood and pasture is what he mainly left them. To those of Sibayo, he gave it to them in the sea, that is in the hills [where] they have their properties, let us say. Each year up until now they go to fish and bring these vegetables: *qochayuyu* ['seaweed'], they say.
>
> The *Inca*, with the *ayllus* of Callalli and above all Sibayo would come down to Chivay. In Chivay, he gave them water. Afterwards, he left them just *sarasenqa*, the waste from maize. That is why they do not have maize in Chivay.
>
> They arrived in Yanque, where the *curacas* were rebels and brave. They almost did not want to respect the *Inca*. For this reason they do not have water [in Yanque]. However, he did leave them [by chance, did he drop it?] a small ear of corn.
>
> Then he descended down to Cabanaconde. In Cabanaconde he left them an intact cob of maize. It is because of this that in Cabanaconde there is so much maize.

This account tells us about the status of the *Inca* above all as a giver of technology. The *Inca* orders the stones, which transform themselves into terraces. He produces water, and gives the people livestock and maize. All these are activities directly related with the redistribution that the *Tawantinsuyu* organized. The myth also describes the ecological conditions of the area; the place where the *Inca* distributes livestock and grasses is the *puna* of Sibayo and Callalli, at around 4,000 meters, while the distribution of maize takes place in Cabanaconde, where the climate is appropriate and where I also collected other oral accounts which deal with the organization of an Inca *mitta* for the mass production of maize. An important feature of this account is that Yanque is the highest point where maize is grown in the valley.

Under the inevitable influence of the European perspectives of the era, the chroniclers transformed the *Inca* into a European king, who acceded to power via a hereditary system based on primogeniture and the legitimacy originating from a monogamous marriage among "brothers and sisters". Each *Inca* appeared in the chronicles as a chief of a *panaqa* or kinship group of the Cusco elite, and it should be understood that these all functioned simultaneously. The Inca was designated through a complex ritual by which the Sun (*Inti*) nominated him. The Andean chronicler Feilpe Guamán Poma de Ayala stated: "In order to be king, Cápac Apo Ynga had to be called in the temple by his father, the Sun, who named him to be king and they did not look to see if he was older or younger, but rather to see who had been chosen by the Sun." Other Spanish chroniclers coincided in the view that the quality of being the *Inca* was ascertained through a ritual designation in which divinity was manifested. The *Inca* was thus a god who should be carried on a litter as the divine strength that emanated from him could cause catastrophes if his power should enter into contact with the earth. It is difficult, given the current state of research, to adequately relate this image of the *Inca* with the sources regarding the duality of Andean authority.

The ritual of the *Inca's* journeys can be fully appreciated in the following description by Francisco Xerez, who published his *True Relation of the Conquest of Peru and the Province of Cusco Called New Castille* in 1534. Xerez stated that when Atahualpa was going to enter the main square in Cajamarca, where he was taken prisoner by the Spaniards, he was preceded by:

> A squadron of Indians dressed in a livery of checkered colors [that is, with squares, like a chessboard]. They came removing the straw from the ground and sweeping the path. After these came another three squadrons dressed in a different style, all singing and dancing. Then came many people with armor, patens and crowns of gold and silver. Among these, came Atabilapa in a litter lined with parrot feathers of many colors, garnished with badges of gold and silver.

Other descriptions of the era add trumpeters to the scene. In this way, the journeys of the *Inca* were clearly a complex ritual, understandable only through their sacred status.

The *Inca* appeared in the chronicles as a mediator on a grand scale, intervening as such in ethnic conflicts. In this way, the *Inca* behaved just like a *curaca*, albeit at a superior level. The *Inca* mediates and negotiates with the other Andean gods, since the myths collected by certain authors in the central mountains of Peru, especially by the cleric Francisco de Avila, a well-known extirpator of Andean "idolotries", present him negotiating with other divinities, arranging alliances, requesting and offering help for the conquests. Throughout his expeditions in Andean territory, related in the chronicles, the *Inca* also appears distributing goods of the highest value and prestige among the population, for example, woolen clothing, maize, coca and *mullu*.

The chronicles allow glimpses of the fact that the government of the *Inca* had brought to the Andes a form of *pax incaica*. This is relative; what appears most probable is a continuous tension between the consensus achieved through redistribution and the conflict that would happen when it did not function. This is a point which requires greater research.

The *Inca* married women of the different Cusco kinship groups, and the chronicles emphasize that the "principal wife" or *Coya* came from the same group or *panaqa* as the ruler. As a result, she was considered his sister. But the *Inca* also married women from other ethnic groups incorporated into the *Tawantinsuyu*. This was a way of becoming kin with the group and thus generating a specific reciprocal relationship.

The Inca (or at least, his ideal conceptualization) was a symbol of the *Tawantinsuyu* for the chroniclers and, certainly, the origin of various forms of life, according to the oral traditions of the Andean population, who considered him one of the original gods. After the 16th century, he was transformed into a messianic hero, on whose resurrection depended the restoration of the Andean cosmos which had disintegrated as a result of the Spanish invasion.

The Cusco Elite

The chroniclers were very concerned with establishing the presence of an Inca nobility and, equally as in other cases, they presented it in a European manner. "Nobles" are, in the chronicles, those who are related to the ruler or his predecessors, an understanding which transformed into nobles all members of the Cusco *panaqas* as each *Inca* gave rise to the formation of one of these groups. But in Cusco not just were there *panaqas*, there were also *ayllus*, which makes us think of another form of hierarchy. The *panaqas* were the following:

1)	Chima panaca	Manco Cápac
2)	Raura panaca	Sinchi Roca
3)	Hauayñin panaca	Lloque Yupanqui
4)	Usca Mayta panaca	Mayta Cápac
5)	Apu Mayta panaca	Cápac Yupanqui
6)	Vicaquirao panaca	Inca Roca
7)	Aucaylli panaca	Yahuar Huaca
8)	Sucsu panaca	Viracocha
9)	Iñaca panaca	Pachacuti
10)	Cápac Ayllu	Tupa Inca Yupanqui
11)	Tumipampa	Huayna Cápac

This list, as well as the relationships between the *panaqas* and the list of *Coyas* or "principal women" of the Incas, entails without doubt many problems since it is possible to argue whether the *panaqas* are originally simultaneous or whether, as the chronicles prefer to assert, they appeared in sequence as a consequence of the accession to power of each *Inca*.

The members of the *panaqas* formed the Cusco or Inca elite but it can also be said that every resident of the city also formed it as Cusco was a sacred city which offered this status to anyone who lived there. This point is recognized not just by the chroniclers but also by subsequent authors, including those of the 18th century. The chroniclers distinguished between those members born to the elite (relatives of the *Incas*, belonging to the *panaqas* and known as nobles "by blood") and those known as "Incas by privilege", who had been ennobled by the *Inca* as reward for their service. It might also be better to distinguish between those who belonged to *panaqas* (royal *ayllus*) and those who formed part of the Cusco *ayllus* which were not categorized as *panaqa*, as well as those that were incorporated into the elite of each ethnic group that came under Inca dominion. These would comprise the bureaucracy and would be in charge of the functions of the expanding *Tawantinsuyu*.

It is worth recalling the names of the functionaries most frequently mentioned in the chronicles: *Tocricuc* (Inca regional governor); *Michiq* (identified by the chroniclers as the governor's lieutenant); *Tucuyricuc* (a functionary who acted, according to the chroniclers, like an inspector or "eyes and ears of the *Inca*" as he travelled to different regions of the *Tawantinsuyu*. He did not just gather information but also had authority to resolve problems and local conflicts); finally, the *Quipucamayuq*, identified as a specialist in the management of the quipus or accounting instruments. Naturally, the chroniclers frequently identified the Inca functionaries with their Spanish equivalents.

Other functionaries or "specialists" of a different nature were the *Cápaq Ñan Tocricuc*, charged with the administration of the roads of the *Tawantinsuyu*. They can be thought of as the managers of its construction and maintenance. We should also not forget to mention the *Qollqa Kamayuq*, charged with the administration of the storehouses.

The chronicles mention similar other functionaries, such as those charged with looking after the bridges on the Inca roads. All these roles appear, however, to be incorporated into the *mitta* regime. There also existed messengers or *chasquis*. These delivered messages by running along the roads, with calculated daily distances and network of posts, for which there were *tampu*, possibly distinct from those that were used to house provisions for the lodging of travelers and troops. In the lodgings for the *chasquis* there were personnel on permanent duty. The chroniclers indicate that there was also one type of *chasqui* for bringing fresh fish from the sea to the ruler of Cusco. It is not known if these were the same people who brought news or orders. The *chasquis* kept fulfilling their functions until long after the Spanish invasion.

One type of very special functionary was the *amauta*, whom the chronicles describe as a master or learned man specialized in teaching the elite, although some sources describe him similarly to seers or certain types of priest. The *amauta* exercised his functions in the *Yachaywasi*, a term frequently translated as "school" in the chronicles. Linked without doubt to teaching, the existence of official historians is also mentioned who transmitted oral memory, possibly in a ritual manner. The chronicles indicate that on the accession of each new ruler, they would relate the extravagant acts of the preceding ruler.

It can be concluded that during the expansion of the *Tawantinsuyu* the *curacas* did not automatically form part of the Inca administration, although it is evident that they were related to it. In fact, in some well documented regions a visible difference can be appreciated between those *curacas* who made up a special category of the elite, linked with the *Inca* himself (such as the *curacas* of Chucuito, on the southeastern bank of Titicaca) and other neighboring ethnic lords who did not always enjoy the same prerogatives. Nor is it evident that all the *curacas* were appointed by the *Inca*. There is sufficient evidence to establish the opposite; that the forms of access to ethnic power did not depend on the rule of Cusco but on the constant and established rules of each ethnic group. At most, it can be said that the *Inca* "confirmed" the ethnic decisions which had previously been brought before him. This confirmation was a ritual.

There was a marked difference between the members of the Cusco elite belonging to the *panaqas*, known to the chroniclers as "big ears" as they wore flaps on their ears as a symbol of their special rank, and the members of the local ruling classes. Among the latter we must distinguish between those who were fully integrated into the *Tawantinsuyu* and those who were not, possibly for having been submitted following a bloody conflict or for having rebelled against the *Inca*. Finally, it should be emphasized that the Inca administration and that of the *curacas* was convergent and functioned along the same principles; for example, the managing of reciprocities and the administration of redistribution.

With the expansion of the *Tawantinsuyu* the influence of the non-Cusco local elites must have grown along with an increase in the forms of incorporation into the administrative mechanics of the Incas. The final moments of the Inca conquests coincide with an increase in the workforce dedicated permanently to the central power (the *yanacuna* of the *Inca*, for example) and it is possible, as some authors such as J.V. Murra have suggested, that in the final days of the *Tawantinsuyu*, the *yanas* began to carry a different weight given that their numbers had grown and, as a consequence, the amount of human energy available to power had grown. It is also notable that the local elites (whose organization, other than that of the *curacazgos*, remains uncertain) could enter into conflict with the central elite of Cusco, as appears to have happened in the war between Huáscar and Atahualpa, which was taking place exactly when the Spaniards arrived in the Andes.

The Curaca: Ethnic Lord

The chronicles of the 16th century speak of the *curacas* using the name "*caciques*", employing a word from the Caribbean that had arrived in the Andes via Mexico, and they identified them in the feudal manner as "lords of vassals". From this point, much confusion arose regarding the *curacas* since the chroniclers also mentioned that they were appointed or confirmed by the *Inca* of Cusco. Sources of the same chroniclers as well as other documents from the 16th century specify more clearly that, in general, the *curacas* were appointed through a ritual procedure within their own ethnic group and that, once in their official posts, they were regarded as sacred. For this reason, they were carried on litters and they were connected to the *huacas*. Their movements were also undertaken within a complex ritual similar to that for the *Inca*. It does not appear correct, therefore, that all the *curacas* were functionaries of the *Tawantinsuyu*, and it is possible that the image of a weighty bureaucracy presented in the chronicles may actually be the transposition of a general tendency in the growing Spanish empire of the 16th century.

It is clear that the authority of the *curaca* extended over his ethnic group, even though there were two authorities for each ethnic group, with a *hanan curaca* and an *urin curaca*. But there were also lesser ethnic authorities that were also known as *curacas* for smaller entities such as *parcialidades* and *cabeceras*, as important towns were known in the 16th century. The chronicles presented a hierarchy of administrative authorities organized decimally:

Pisca Camáyoc	5 familias
Chunca Camáyoc	10 familias
Pisca Chunca Camáyoc	50 familias
Pachaca Camáyoc	100 familias
Pisca Pachaca Camáyoc	500 familias
Guaranca Camáyoc	1000 familias
Pisca Guaranca Camáyoc	5000 familias
Hunu Camáyoc	10000 familias

This list of authorities has been presented as the fundamental base of a bureaucratic structure, and some authors say that the term *curaca* was used for the head of 100 families. However, it appears more certain that this relationship [the unit of 100 families] was used more for calculating the population, something which was fundamental for the *mitta*, than as part of the administrative hierarchy. The colonial inspections of the 16th century allow us to see that the halves that existed at the level of the ethnic group were not necessarily equivalent to the size of the population. The term *camáyoc* (*Kamayuq* in Quechua) refers to any authority at the point when it is exercising specific functions.

It was previously mentioned that not all *curacas* were appointed through a ritual within their own group. There was another type of *curaca* which did directly form part of the administrative structure of the Incas. This was the case for those who regulated the Inca *mitmaqkuna* or those who had authority over the groups of *yanas* (dependents of an authority, in this case the *Inca*). There are even documented situations in which a *yana* of the *Inca* functioned as the authority over a population which was not *yana*, and it is evident that the frontier garrisons had authorities appointed by the central government of Cusco. The documentation of the 16th century presents the *curacas* of each half of an ethnic group as being of around the same age. This is only possible if the two *curacas*, corresponding to each half or faction, were chosen at the same time, in such a way that the death of one of the two *curacas* of the group would lead to both being replaced, with the surviving member of the original pair of *curacas* in a special situation, possibly as the supreme mediator or counselor within the group.

It is not totally clear if all the *curacas* exercised their authority over the storehouses organized by the Inca administration. But it is evident that they administered those that relied on the internal *mittas* of the group. It is possible that in the great administrative centers founded by the *Tawantinsuyu* for the practice of redistribution, there were functionaries specialized in the control of the *mitta* that took place there, in the same way as specialists in accounting, *khipukamayuq*, who were in charge of registering everything that entered and left the storehouses.

The *curaca*, in sum, is more clearly identified with ethnic authority, including functions such as the administration of communal goods (*sapsi*) and the control of human energy employed for redistributive purposes, for which they organized, for example, the tasks necessary to gather resources from distant or ecologically distinct areas. The *curaca* also mediated between the different family groups incorporated into the reciprocal mechanics and, apparently, kept account of the reciprocities, intervening in order to resolve any differences arising from reciprocal relationships and obligations. The authority of the *curaca* derived fundamentally from his religious function, which led him to preside over rituals and ceremonies, such as serving as an intermediary with the local divinities, thus leading agricultural and other ceremonies that made up the sacred calendar of the population. Finally, during the *Tawantinsuyu*, the *curaca* served as a medium of communication between the Cusco authorities and his own group. This function explains why the *Inca* sought to marry into the *curacas'* families in such a way as to generate reciprocal ties between them.

Inca and Local Administration

The chronicles leave the impression of a highly centralized Inca administration, which functioned across the entire, extensive territory of the *Tawantinsuyu*. As they were writing for readers who were principally, if not entirely, European, the chroniclers must have sought to offer an image of the Americas, in this case the Andes, that could easily fit within the concepts and categories that Europeans then knew. As a result, they did not just present a monarchical government, organized along European lines, but they also claimed the existence of a royal council, which some chroniclers wrote was comprised of the chiefs of each *suyu*, each of which was known as *Suyuyuc Apu* ("Lord" of a *suyu*), and assimilated in the chronicles into the figure of a Spanish viceroy. Others, such as Guamán Poma, indicated the existence of a council constituted by 12 members and presided by two *Incas*, one from *hanan* Cusco and one from *urin* Cusco. Four members corresponded to Chinchaysuyu, several others to Collasuyu, two to Antisuyu and, finally, two to Cuntisuyu. Guamán Poma noted that the council was similar in its functions to the Council of Castille, that is to say that it was a body of administrators and advisors of the highest level of Inca power.

Each *suyu* had been ruled by a dependent authority of the *Inca*, who was in charge of the *Hunu Camáyoc* who ruled groups of one thousand families. A satisfactory explanation has yet to be found for this system organized around the decimal division of the population, and today it is suggested that this system's purpose was more clearly related to keeping a population census than administration.

But the chronicles and colonial documents reveal other information of interest to our understanding of how the *Tawantinsuyu* was administered. The organizational base kept functioning those *curacas* and ethnic groups incorporated in the "Empire of the Incas", submitted as they were to an organization which the chroniclers assumed to be centralized, comprised principally by members of the Cusco elite. The most notable element is that the axis of this administration revolved around control of human energy, which made possible the redistribution exercised by power. The *curacas* actively intervened in this. In the same manner as the *curacas* but on a grander scale, the *Inca* had to be "generous" and distribute essential goods among the population. This required increasing quantities of manual labor and the early colonial documents tell us that contributions to the *Inca* consisted in people dedicated to carrying out specific tasks. For example, in Huánuco, the *curacas* provided in 1549 the following information regarding what the Chupaychu ethnic group handed over to the *Inca*:

> On being asked in the time of the Yngas [sic] what Indians were thrown into the gold mines, they said that of every 100 Indians, they threw three Indian men and three Indian women and they spent the whole year digging [gold] and that this gold was taken to Cusco and likewise 60 Indian men and 60 Indian women were digging for silver the whole year and they dug for it in Yaros and theY took it to Cusco.

> On being asked what continuous service said province of the Chupachos made to the *Ynga* in Cusco and outside of it, they said that 400 Indian men and women stayed continuously in Cusco to make walls and if someone died they provided another.

> Plus they gave 400 Indians to sow *chacras* in Cusco so that people could eat and make their homes.

> Plus for the *yanaconas* of Guaynacava 150 Indians continuously.

> Plus for the bodyguard of Topa Ynga Yupangue after his death 150 Indians continuously.

> Plus for guarding his weapons 10 *yanaconas*.

> Plus for the guard of Chachapoyas 200 Indians.

> Plus for the guard of Quito 200 Indians.

> Plus for the bodyguard of Guaynacava after his death 20 Indians.

> Plus to make feathers 120 Indians.

> Plus to get honey 60 Indians.

> Plus they gave for Cumbicus 400 Indians.

Plus for making dyes and colors 40 Indians.

Plus for guarding the sheep, 240 Indians.

Plus they gave to guard the chacras that they had in all this valley 40 Indians and most of the maize from there was taken to Cusco and the rest to the storehouses.

Plus they gave 40 Indians to sow chilies which they took to Cusco.

Plus they gave to make salt 60 Indians several times and a few other times 40 and 50.

Plus they gave 60 Indians to make coca, which they brought to Cusco and the storehouses of Guánuco and sometimes they took 200 sacks and sometimes 40.

Plus they gave 40 Indians to go with the person of the Ynga and take deer.

Plus they gave 40 Indians to make soles and they took these to Cusco and the storehouses.

Plus they gave 40 carpenters to make plates and bowls and other things for the Ynga and they brought these to Cusco.

Plus they gave 40 potters to make pots and they took these to Guánuco.

Plus they gave 68 Indians to carry loads from Tanto to Bonbón and from Sutin Cancha to Tambo.

Plus they gave 40 Indians to guard the Ynga's Indian women.

Plus they gave to go with the person of the Ynga and for the hammocks 500 Indians and they went to Quito and other places.

Plus they gave 500 Indians to sow and other things without leaving their lands.

This clear list gives us information about what human energy was provided to the Inca to meet specific tasks, which underscores that the population did not give over any item of their personal production.

But additionally, there is another important question: We must distinguish between those tasks which were permanent and those which could be completed in a brief period or occasionally. This is important because the number of people involved in this list is greater than that of "heads of family units", whom the Chucpaychu ethnic group had in "tributary" status. This list also gives clues that the *curacas* were in charge of the administration of this workforce, except in those cases where it was sent to Cusco or other places. The administration of the central storehouses could thus be distinguished from those situated within ethnic territory. However, the *Inca's* storehouses were not all located in Cusco but were distributed across the Andean area, for example in the administrative centers of Huánuco Pampa, mentioned in the document. In these administrative centers it is evident the existence of people permanently dedicated to the administration of the workforce that worked there (*mittani*) and the vigilance of the center itself and its stores. We have already mentioned that the existence of a large bureaucracy is debatable, but there is no doubt that a large part of the Cusco elite carried out administrative tasks, as the chronicles indicate.

The Population and Population Policy

Demographic calculations for the Andean area prior to the Spanish invasion have varied substantially. Initially, it was thought that the number of habitants of the *Tawantinsuyu* had been low, but the most recent research calculates between approximately nine million and 15 million inhabitants, although the figure could be even higher. All calculations are approximate given that they are made on the basis of estimates made during the early Colony and the decline in the population originating in the demographic crisis which devastated the Andes from the 16th century.

The chronicles mention that Andean society was administered by the *Tawantinsuyu* in such a way that it could mobilize members of the population to achieve a better distribution in line with the resources that each region was able to provide. The chronicles agree that those people transplanted from their places of origin to new zones were known as *mitmaqkuna*. The chronicles also distinguish between the *mitmaqkuna* arising from the need to populate a region and better exploit its resources from those groups within the population mobilized with the strategic purpose of frontier colonization or to occupy areas that perhaps had only recently been incorporated into the *Tawantinsuyu*, or that had seen uprisings, and therefore needed to be in contact with people "more loyal" to the central power and who could also serve as a positive element of control. This did not exclude the simultaneous presence of military garrisons. It is difficult to calculate the number of *mitmaqkuna*, which surely varied according to their political or economic function. The *mitmaqkuna* were not a creation of the Incas. Prior to them, the various ethnic groups kept varying numbers of *mitmaqkuna* in different areas and it is possible that many of them were used to maintain control over zones distant from the nuclear centers of each ethnic group, and in which they carried out agricultural tasks as these ecological "colonies" were destined to diversify production.

If the *mitmaqkuna* sent by the ethnic groups undertook activities principally related to ecological control, those who depended on the *Tawantinsuyu* had broader functions, some of which have already been detailed. All were separated from their kinship groups but it is probable the first ones maintained relationships with their origins and even their rights to redistribution. Instead, the *mitmaqkuna* of the *Inca* appear to have constituted important communities of transplanted members of the population, who, even after the Spanish invasion, maintained their identification as *mitmas* of the *Inca*, forming groups distinct from the rest of the population.

Another type of population transplanted or extracted from the ethnic groups were the *yanakuna*, who the chronicles casually identified as slaves. The existence of *yanas* from the ethnic groups has been proven, and they were responsible for specific productive tasks which required their fulltime attention. Recently, it has been proposed that the root word *yana* is more related to interdependence (*yanantin* thus means "opposite and complementary") than to a relation of dependence similar to slavery. According to this theory, *yana* implies a situation in which an interdependence is exercised under the patterns of reciprocity. If this is correct, relations of this type could have been symmetrical or asymmetrical as in the case of the reciprocity just mentioned. If a *yana* depends on reciprocity, this can be considered part of the temporary obligations either while the reciprocal obligation lasts or in the time it takes to be completed. This would be valid for certain relationships within the ethnic groups, even though the best sources speak of *yanakuna* provided to the *curacas* for the fulfillment of various tasks, including shepherding. The *yanas* who depended on the *curacas*, and especially those who depended on the central authority of the *Tawantinsuyu* thus corresponded to the asymmetrical reciprocity and were, in this case, permanent.

The *yanas* submitted to authority fulfilled the tasks that were assigned to them. It has been pointed out that during the final years of the *Tawantinsuyu* their numbers rose, and we know that some of them were dedicated to cultivating the maize-producing lands of the valley of Yucay, an important area whose produce was destined to feed the Cusco *panaqas*, even though at least of some it was dedicated to the redistribution exercised by the Inca. Despite this, specialists have calculated a low proportion of *yanas* in the time of the *Tawantinsuyu* (one percent in the case of the Lupaqa of Chucuito, although it should be understood that these figures refer to an ethnic group and not to the *Tawantinsuyu* itself). Finally, the *yanas* appear to have been considered as "specialists" and, as much as they depended directly on power, they could always be transferred under the control of distant regions. The *yanas* of Yucay, for example, came from the distant zone of Cañar, in present day Ecuador.

The *yanas* did not only carry out this kind of work. There were also *yanas* who were *curacas* and functionaries. This explains the complexity of the term and its variable reach. In fact, the chroniclers indicate that the *Inca* often distributed *aqlla* or chosen women to his *yanas*. One can thus see that the relationship of the *yana* did not prevent a high social status and, as has been said, any dependent of Cusco authority, including functionaries, could consider themselves a *yana* of the *Inca*. Certainly, the *yanas* of the *Inca* could even be considered privileged within the system, given that they were excluded from all other obligations and were kept by the Cusco apparatus in a direct form.

It is evident that various factors and elements of control influenced Inca population policy. Among these, the seasonal movements of the population destined to complete the *mitta* of the *Tawantinsuyu* stands out. Previously, I mentioned situations such as that arising from the gigantic Inca *mitta* organized in Cochabamba, in which participated members of diverse groups from the Peruvian-Bolivian *alitplano* whose work was linked to the sowing of maize. In these kinds of cases we should also include *mitmakquna* from diverse groups, those who remained in Cochabamba to guard the seeds and control the stores. Among the elements of control for the workforce's movements we should consider the *khipu,* explained in the previous chapter.

The chronicles of the 16th century give early evidence of the *aqlla*, generally qualified as "chosen women" of the Sun or the *Inca*. With the institution thus defined by the early chroniclers, they describe how these were handed over to the Spaniards (possibly to initiate reciprocity relations derived from new kinship relationships, although the Spaniards received them as simple gifts). At the same time, the chroniclers characterized them as a type of nun. The chronicles mention that the *aqlla* were used for various religious functions and that "secondary women" of the *Inca* were chosen from among them. Likewise, the *Inca* could choose to distribute some of them to members of the elite, victorious generals or even those *curacas* he wanted to privilege. The ritual role of the *aqlla* is not discussed but it is clear that they were disconnected from their kinship groups. See, for example, the description of them by Hernando de Santillán in his *Relation of the Origin, Descent, Policy and Government of the Incas* written in 1563:

> [in each ethnic group, the Incas] took many of the most important women, daughters of lords and their brothers and sisters, and others intended for the Sun, those whom they preferred, whom they called "induguarmi" [*Inti warmi* or "women of the Sun"]. He sent them to make home, where they were in much confinement with their guards. They were there always making clothing and other services for the Sun. And others applied to the *guacas* for the same order. And those who applied were also sent to make home, and they gave service and ordered them to make clothing for his person and to his measure. These were called *mamaconas*. It was never permitted to marry any of them. The *Inca* provided everything they needed for their tributes. Of the other women who were of a lesser kind, he chose those who looked best and kept them in another house he ordered built. These he called "agros" [*sic*, for *aqllas*], which means chosen ones. They gave him their service and they were kept isolated, and he also ordered that they make clothing for his person, and of these he gave some women to those he wanted to show mercy, which he always did with those who were his servants and *yanaconas*, even though they had other women.

Santillán allows us to see the characteristics of the *aqlla*, even though only one type of the "chosen women" was thus known. He describes the different functions they had, insisting not just on their separation from their groups of origin (which made them dependent on the resources of the Inca, similarly to those people employed for redistribution) but also highlighting their tasks with textiles, which could not be divorced from the redistribution that the *Inca* exercised as the chronicles tell of multiple "gifts" of clothes that the ruler made, and even the sharing out of these that he made during his conquests and travels across the territory of the *Tawantinsuyu*. There is a discrepancy among the informants of the chroniclers, since although some say that the *aqlla* wove, others, such as Pedro Pizarro (1571), mention that they only sewed as weaving was a job for men. Their dependence on authority converted the *aqlla* into something very similar to the *yanakuna*. As Santillán stated, the *aqlla* could be used as women of the *yanas* of the *Inca*.

Chapter V
Description of Cusco

The chronicles offered successive descriptions from the 16th century of Cusco, its temples and palaces, in which they continually underlined the importance the city held. All the descriptions of the chronicles are important, although they do not always offer us correct information regarding the historic evolution of the city. Archaeology has taken us many steps along this path, although it should be made clear that, attributing 100 years of existence to the *Tawantinsuyu* of the Incas, it is not always possible to arrive at an adequate chronology of the construction of the sacred city of the Incas.

Yet there are different problems regarding the urban design of Cusco, which are not uniquely derived from the modern modifications of the city. In first place, the Inca city was destroyed shortly after the Spanish invasion, during the rebellion headed by Manco Inca in 1536. On that occasion the roofs of the city were set alight and we do not know exactly the extent of the damage. In second place, from the very moment of the Spanish occupation of the city, the urban terrain was distributed among the Spaniards who took up residence there. In this way, parts of the urban area were given to Spaniards who modified them to meet their own needs. A third consideration is that from the first moments of the Spanish occupation activities were undertaken that drastically modified the urban layout of the city; for example, the great central square (comprised of Aucaypata and Cusipata, both separated from the Huatanay River) was altered, with a block of houses erected between the Aucaypata and Cusipata sectors. Finally, and in fourth place, the urban design was clearly changed as the streets were widened and buildings were demolished to adapt the spaces to a new urban use.

A distinct problem is the absence of city maps from the 16th century that would have made it possible to develop a better knowledge of Inca Cusco. Various modern authors have sought to reconstruct the original urban layout of Cusco using as a basis the surviving Inca walls, but it is obvious that the widening of the streets could have involved the displacing of these walls, which could have been reconstructed using the same techniques, as Dr. John H. Rowe has personally communicated to me. In fact, contemporary authors have noted that the views of the city, printed in different works since the 16th century, correspond to imaginary visions where the urban layouts have been elaborated, at least in part, in line with the accounts of the chroniclers, but giving the constructions clear characteristics of the European architecture of those times.

The vagueness of the chronicles gives rise to other problems. I previously mentioned that the Incas built "other Cuscos", specifically identified with the administrative centers of the Incas, and placed in distinct locations within the Andean area. Archaeologists have shown that the plans of some of these, perhaps all, do not correspond to those of Inca Cusco. This is due to the fact that the Incas based the similarity of the administrative centers with Cusco on the gathering of certain basic elements symbolically grouped together: *ushnu*, *aqllawasi*, ("palace of the *Inca*", Valcárcel would say), and, we should add, the storehouses or *qollqa*. These elements configured a symbolic whole that identified the Incas and their administrative centers, which were, therefore, "the same as" Cusco.

Some chronicles of the Cusco cycle, among which the works of Cieza de León, Betanzos, Sarmiento de Gamboa y Molina stand out, called attention to the way the foundation of Cusco by the first *Inca*, Manco Capac, had been associated with the organization of a system to drain the "wetlands" that occupied the site. They likewise stated that the early city was built between the Tulumayo and Huatanay Rivers. It has been frequently said that the Inca city had the shape of a puma whose head was comprised of the fort of Sacsaywaman, body lay between the two rivers, and whose tail was likewise located in a place called Pumaq Chupan. An engraving in which these figure can be found appears in the book of Ephraim George Squier, *Incidents of Travel and Explorations in the Land of the Incas* (1877), although the subject has been studied by subsequent authors (see Rowe, Chávez, Ballón, Gasparini-Margolies). The definitive structure of the city is attributed by the chronicles to two moments in the time of the Incas, the first being that of Pachacuti, who rebuilt the city after the war with the Chancas, according to the chronicles, and the second, it is said, the important modifications that occurred during the time of the government of Huayna Cápac.

The chroniclers also highlighted the symbolic meaning of Cusco as the center and origin of the world of the Incas. The city itself was revered and became a symbol of the *Tawantinsuyu* itself. This explains the symbolic repetition of the structure of the city in the Inca administrative centers. One chronicler even stated that whoever was coming from Cusco should be the subject of reverence by whoever was going there, given that he had been in contact with the sacred city. Even in the 18th century Ignacio de Castro was able to write, along the lines of Inca Garcilaso de la Vega:

Those Indians who inhabit it, as well as those who came there [the city of Cusco] from elsewhere held it in such esteem and veneration that it even bordered on being a religious cult the estimation that they had for it. Their inhabitants, products, habits and customs, their manners were considered with I do not know what kind of divine glaze, in other words because in their reduced intelligence [that of Andean men] their sovereigns were not different from Gods whom they adored as descendants of the same divinities, so that they saw the city as Temple of these Semi-Gods. Or for this general ailment of the dominant courts and cities that did not exalt but that which is fruit of the vicinity; looking at the provinces, its men and works with this concern that is caused by proximity to the Sovereign.

One of those who accompanied Francisco Pizarro on his voyage from Cajamarca to Cusco was Pedro Sancho, Pizarro's secretary and author of a *Relation of the Conquest of Peru*, unknown in Spanish until the last century, even though there were prior editions in Italian and English. Sancho gave a first description of the city:

The city of Cusco, for being the first of all those where the lords had their residence, is so great and lovely that it would be worthy of being seen even in Spain, and all of it full of lords' palaces, because in it poor people do not live, and each lord constructs in it his house and likewise all the *caciques* even those that do not live there continuously. The greater part of these houses is of stone. There are many houses of adobe and they are very well ordered, with streets made in the form of a cross, very straight, all paved, and down the middle of each one runs a water pipe made of stone. The problem they have is that of being narrow, because on one side of the pipe can pass just one man on a horse, and another on the other side. This city is placed on the low-point of a mountain and there are many houses on its side and others in the plain below. The square is square and in the main flat, and paved with pebbles. Around it there are four houses of the lords who are the principal ones of the city, painted and worked in stone, and the best of them is the house of the old Guaynacava *cacique*, and the door is of soft marble and raised and of other colors, and it has other buildings with terraced roofs, very worthy of being seen. There are in this city many lodgings and grandees. They pass along both sides of the rivers that are born a league above Cusco and from there until two leagues below the city, all is paved so that the water runs clean and clear and even though it grows it does not break its banks. They have their bridges for those who enter the city. On the hill, which at the location of the city is round and very rough, there is a fort of earth and very beautiful stone. Within it there are many lodgings and a principal tower in the middle made in the style of a cube, with four or five parts, one on top of another. The lodgings and rooms within are tiny, and the stones of which it is made are very well worked, and so well adjusted to each other that there appears to be no merging, and the stones are so smooth that they appear planed planks, with the join ordered, in the custom of Spain, one against the other. There are so many rooms and towers that a person cannot see everything in one day, and many Spaniards that have seen it and have been in Lombardy and in other strange kingdoms say that they have not seen another building as strong as this fort, nor castle. There could be five thousand Spaniards inside. They cannot be attacked with artillery nor can they be tunneled out because it is placed on a stone outcrop. Of the part of the city that is a very rough hill, there is not more than one nearby. Of the part that is less rough, there are three, one higher than the other, and the last one more inside, is the highest of all. The most beautiful thing that there can be among buildings of that land are those nearby, because they are of stones so large that nobody that sees them will not say that they were placed there by human hands, that they are so large like pieces of mountains or large crags, that there are ones 30 palms high and others as long and others of 20 and 25, and others of 15 but there is not one of them so small that it may be carried by three carts. These are not smooth stones, but very well fitted and worked one to the other [...]´.

Pedro Sancho's text is very eloquent. It does not just indicate the generic lines of the city but also highlights the strength of Sacsaywaman, in the description of which he lingers, noting certain characteristics that the subsequent chroniclers would repeat regarding the stonemasonry, its size and the form of its joints. The subsequent descriptions, including those of our days, testify to the gradual modification, not just of the urban layout of Cusco and its buildings, but also that of the fortress, many of whose stones were used for the urban constructions of Spanish Cusco.

Some of Sancho's claims stand out: He states that the streets were "in the form of a cross", something which was seen as important in the Spanish constructions of the era. However, Cusco does not have the shape of a "checkerboard" (divided into squares) even though its streets tend to be straight in certain sectors. Naturally, the chronicler criticizes the narrowness of the streets, intended for pedestrians, while the Spaniards conceived of them for riding horses. For that, it did not appear sufficient that the streets only allowed one horse to pass on each side of the sewer. The description of the square is important, surrounded as it was by "palaces" built by the Incas. These were Quishar Cancha, frequently referenced as the temple dedicated to the "maker" (Wiraqocha or Pachayachachi), the Cuyusmanco, where the present day cathedral of Cusco and Church of the Triumph are found, the place where the Spaniards were garrisoned during the siege of the city during the rebellion of Manco Inca (1536), and finally Cassana, frequently mentioned as the palace of Pachacuti. The chroniclers also indicated that not all the area referred to as Cusco was actually built up, but it is notable in the description of Pedro Sancho that part of the city had stone buildings and part adobe buildings. This chronicler indicated that in Cusco there were no "poor people", by which he meant that the entire population of the city belonged to the elite.

The central square of the city had another notable characteristic. Juan Polo de Ondegardo, one of the most zealous Andean researchers of the 16th century, states that in Cusco's main square:

[...]they removed the very soil and brought it to other places as a thing of great esteem, and they filled it with sand from the seacoast up to two and a half palms, in some places more. They sowed all over it cups of gold and silver, small ewes and small figurines made of the same, of which there was a great quantity, which we have all seen. Of this sand was the whole square [covered] when I came to govern that city, and if it is true that that sand was brought from where they affirm and have in their registries, it appears to me that all the earth together needed to be brought in that same way, because the square is large and it is without number the loads that entered into it [...].

Polo de Ondegardo stated that he had therefore needed an enormous workforce to fill the square of Cusco with sand. At the same time, when Polo recounts how the earth of the main square of Cusco was taken to other cities founded by the Incas, it should be understood that this was the case particularly with the administrative centers created by the activity of Inca power in different places in the Andes. This occurred because the earth of Cusco was sacred, and on bringing earth from the city, the creation of a new sacred space was determined which enjoyed the same characteristics of the city of Cusco. For this reason, the administrative centers thus founded were called "other Cuscos" in the chronicles and it was stated that certain buildings constructed in the Cusco manner (*aqllawasi* or "palace of the Inca", *ushnu* or "solar temple" etc.) formed part of this condition.

Likewise, Cusco was described by the chroniclers as a symbolic center of the land of the Incas, as well as the place where the four principal roads headed out to each of the four *suyu* which together formed the "the four parts of the world". Ever since the chroniclers, the *suyu* have frequently been identified with two roads that were directed towards them, considering these as an axis around which the *suyu* would develop. This image of the chroniclers referred to the significance that roads would acquire in the organization of the *Tawantinsuyu* of the Incas.

Regarding the urban organization of Cusco, a long list of temples has been known for a long time. This list of *huacas* or *ceques* of Cusco, was initially attributed to Polo de Ondegardo and was completed in the 17th century from diverse sources by P. Bernabé Cobo S. J., who included it in his *History of the New World*, finished around 1653. The text describes in detail Cusco's many sacred places, united very possibly in symbolic form, along imaginary lines or ritual roads known as *ceques*. The text indicates that from the temple of Coricancha:

> [...] came out of the center certain lines that the Indians call *ceques*. And they make four parts in agreement with the four royal paths that came out of Cusco. And in each of these *ceques* there was by his order the *Guacas* and temples that there were in Cusco and its district, as stations of pious places, whose veneration was general for all, and each *ceque* was the charge of the factions, and families of the said city of Cusco [...].

In this way, Chinchaysuyu had nine *ceques*, with 85 *huacas*; Antisuyu counted nine *ceques* and 78 *huaca;*, Collasuyu had nine *ceques* and 85 *huacas;* and finally Cuntisuyu 14 *ceques* and 80 *huacas*. There is still not a satisfactory explanation of this incoherent set of numbers, supposing that the four suyu were symmetrical. Nor is there a correlation with the asymmetry that certain chroniclers, such as Guamán Poma, indicated when they noted that the two *hanan suyu* had twice the number of authorities than the *urin*. Beyond that, there were four *huacas* that belonged to more than one *ceque*.

The system of *ceques* has been employed to explain the dualist image of the organization of Cusco, with the corresponding *ceques* of Chinchaysuyu and Antisuyu understood to be ordered clockwise, while their counterparts, Collasuyu and Cuntisuyu, were ordered counterclockwise. This is based on the fact that the *suyu* were "divided" into Collana, Payán and Cayao sectors, a ternary classification system known in the Andes and highlighted by R.T. Zuidema who studied the *ceques* of Cusco. Other interpretations may also be valid, for example, the reverse interpretation (Cayao, Payán, Collana) would only appear in the part that corresponds to Antisuyu in the list of *huacas* reproduced by P. Cobo (see, for example, Rowe 1985). The *urin* sector (Collasuyu and Cuntisuyu) would have more *ceques* and *huacas* than the *hanan* (Chinchaysuyu and Antisuyu). It is notable that Collana, Payán and Cayao designated a line of greater or lesser importance and prestige, and should be understood that its use in kinship is particularly important. However, the reference to each of these kinship groups must be relative based on the context of the information. These are attributed to "factions", some of which are identified as "royal ayllus" or *panaqa* but which may, with difficulty, be converted from a criterion of social organization or kinship into one of population distribution, since the theoretical distribution of the *panaqas* due to the *ceques* could not be projected onto the urban layout of Cusco.

Chapter VI
The Inca Religion

There are few subjects more controversial than this, as it is one of those topics where the chroniclers came up against significant obstacles to providing relatively impartial accounts. It is has been correctly highlighted that the chroniclers of the 16th century inaugurated the ethnology of the Americas in those times, but although they did try to be objective regarding certain aspects of the material culture, this was not so easy regarding religious issues, given that here they came up against problems originating in an official orthodoxy on which depended not just a conception of life and history but also, fundamentally, that of the notion of a supreme truth centered on divinity. For this reason, the religions of the Americas in general and of the Andes in particular were considered "idolatrous", demoniacal manifestations that had to be uprooted through evangelization.

Andean Cosmovision

From the accounts of the Andean myths incorporated in the chronicles it is possible to arrive at an image of the Inca cosmovision. Both time and space were sacred and undoubtedly had a mythical explanation and a ritual representation. The chronicles are extravagant in their reproduction of myths in which a conception of space is presented that is basically dualist, that is to say, divided into *hanan* and *urin* (or *allauca* and *ichoc, alaasa* and *masaa*, etc.). This should not amaze us given that myths offer information corresponding to the conception of the world and the categories that govern it. Dualism is one of these, through which space was conceived as a sum of realms designed in the ordering of the whole that Wiraqocha conducted in Tiawanaku (*vide supra*). Diego González Holguín, author of one of the first bilingual dictionaries (Spanish-Quechua, edited in 1608) noted that *Tawantinsuyu* meant "all of Peru, or the four parts which are Ante suyu [*sic*], Collasuyu, Conti suyu, Chinchay suyu". Here, "All of Peru" means "all of the world", given that for the Andean peoples "the world" was "all the world", *their world*, in an ethnocentric vision. The term "Peru" in the text of González Holguín is a neologism incorporated following the Spanish invasion, given that it was not used in the Andes until then.

If horizontal space was divided into two parts, each of which was subdivided into another two, the world appeared comprised of three planes: *hanan racha*, "the world above"; *kay pacha*, "the world here"; and *ucu pacha* or *urin pacha*, "the world below". The term *pacha*, which is used for the three planes of the world, may signify at the same time "time" and "space", the final notion in terms of world, earth and place. However, the possibility remains that this may be connected to the transfer of the Christian, European image of the trinity. Possibly, there were two worlds, *hanan pacha* and *urin* [*ucu*] *pacha*. *Kay pacha* may be a place of union and meeting, that is to say, *tinkuy*. *Pachamama* is clearly recognised as the divinity of the earth (the earth mother), producer of food and identified both in the chronicles and in the present day as a small girl; in the middle of the 17th century the Jesuit Bernabé Cobo, for example, mentioned that girls' clothing was offered to Pachamama. Pachamama lives below the earth and inside the mountains and is, therefore, a chthonic divinity.

The places from where people (the kinship groups) originated were always located in the subsoil and were known as *paqarina*.

Opposite Pachamama, in a dualist conception, there must be another divinity or an equivalent divine category belonging to the world above; the only equivalent divinity in the collection of known Andean gods appears to be *Wiraqocha*, who in the chronicles that used sources from the southern area of Peru, between Cusco and Lake Titicaca, is presented as the most important divinity. Wiraqocha corresponds to a type of clearly celestial divinity with solar characteristics. In the myths of Cusco, after realizing a first ordering of the world, sending the sun and moon to the sky, thus creating light, Wiraqocha proceeded to divide the world into four parts: Chinchaysuy, to the west; Collasuyu, to the east; Antisuyu, to the north; and Cuntisuyu, to the south. Subsequently, he ordered men to arise from caves, springs, canyons, that is to say, the subsoil, in the regions of Chinchaysuyu and Collaysuyu, while his "helpers" did his work in Antisuyu and Cuntisuyu. There are two important questions here: a) The interaction between Wiraqocha and Pachamama, which resolves to a large degree the sky-earth duality (k*ay pacha*, the world here, is the result of this connection); b) In second place, Wiraqocha follows the path of the sun, losing himself in the ocean. Wiraqocha appears to have remained "in the sky" or, as one chronicler states, "at the ends of the earth", and his religious importance is presented in the chronicles as less than that of *Inti*, the sun, a divinity that is highlighted by the same authors as being an official divinity of the Incas. Although the most likely scenario is that Wiraqocha was a divinity prior to the Incas, with the advent of the Incas, Inti acquired preeminence. It should be noted, however, that the sun also appears as a partner of Pachamama in other myths.

Despite its widespread use in the Andes, it cannot be said that the term *Pachamama* is the only denomination used for this telluric divinity, which lives in and represents the subsoil. Pachamama is a type of important divinity that exists in the entire region and can have different names. In the same way, gods similar to Wiraqocha exist in other parts of the Andes and their activities relate the earth with the sky. It is possible that many of these gods (*Con* or *Cuniraya*, *Pachacama*, *Tunapa*, etc.) are, in reality, local names for a notion of a divinity similar to Wiraqocha. Some accounts gathered in the present-day department of Lima, on the central coast of Peru, present a similar duality to that of Wiraqocha-Pachamama; the known myth of Wa-Kon, for example, talks of Pachacámac as the husband of the earth, and together they engendered a pair of twins. Pachacámac drowned at sea, and the earth, Pachamama, remained a widow, with her children. Another duality similar to the sky-earth pairing can be appreciated in one of the most important non-Cusco Andean myths, that of Huarochirí, a zone that in the 16th century included a wide extension of the central rainforest of current day Peru. This divine duality was known there as *Cuniraya-Urpayhuachac*; the full name of the first of these two divinities was *Cuniraya Wiraqocha*.

The sky-earth (subsoil) duality entails the search for elements of communication between the two planes of the world. Among the best known, is the beam *Illapa*, and the rainbow frequently associated with the snake *Amaru*. Likewise, the *Inca* was the point of communication between the planes of the world, as he was the son of the Sun (of Wiraqocha in some texts) and he arose from within the earth. In fact, the term *Inca* (or *Enqa* in Aymara) appears to predate the *Tawantinsuyu* and initially be independent of it, although during the *Tawantinsuyu* it reached an undoubted special presence on its transformation into a symbol of the world order and the name of the ruler that maintained that order. Originally, *Inca* appeared to indicate the "first creator", identical to Cámac.

The Andean image of time is cyclical and the chroniclers presented successive ages of the world. Guamán Poma, for example, spoke of four ages prior to the Incas; *Uaricocha runa, Uari runa, Purun runa* and *Auca pacha runa*, during which men would have passed from the time of the first population of the Andes to perfecting agriculture, population growth and the appearance of wars. It has been said that the fourth age appears as a special moment when the ethnic lords reach perfection. The time of the Incas took place in these four ages (*Inca pacha runa*). They imposed themselves on the Andean peoples and inaugurated "idolatry". The men of the first ages were presented by Guamán Poma as: a) Descendants of Noah; and b) In consequence, the possessors of a "true notion of God", the biblical God. Guamán Poma also speaks of five Judeo-Christian ages parallel to the four ages prior to and during the time of the Incas. The last Christian age, the age of Christ, is simultaneous to that of the Incas and can also be considered "outside of time". In reality, Guamán Poma, who finished writing his *New Chronicle and Good Government* around 1615, is clearly influenced by evangelization and, in consequence, needs to incorporate his Andean vision of time into the linear image of history. This explains how the Andean ages are included in his work within a wider framework that can be read in the following way:

Andean Ages		Christian or European Ages	
1.	*Uari Uiracocha runa* (III)	I	Adam and Eve (I)
2.	*Uari runa* (IV)	II	Noah (II)
3.	*Purun runa* (V)	III.	Abraham
4.	*Auca runa* (VI)	IV	David
5	*Inca runa* (VII)	V.	Jesus
6	"Spain in the Indies"	VIII	The Present

After the supposedly parallel ages, Guamán Poma considers a sixth age common to Spain and the Andes, "Spain in the Indies". But it must be understood that the first Andean age, Uari Uiracocha runa, is enacted by the descendants of Noah on their arrival in the Americas. Thus, we would have a distinct enumeration and sequence, placed in parenthesis in the list above. Under this schema, the first Andean age would really be the third in a lineal, integrated conception and "Spain in the Indies" the eighth. In his work, Guamán Poma considers himself a "precursor" of the new coming of Christ, who would constitute a new age of the world, the ninth under Guamán Poma's schema. This cannot be left unremarked because in the lists of the Cusco *Incas*, the ninth place corresponds to Pachacuti, traditionally known in the chronicles as "he who transforms the world", which also has a special ring to it when applied to Christ. Guamán Poma therefore seeks a symbiosis of the ideas of European and Andean time, resolving them without losing sight of the notions incorporated by the evangelization.

In the myths compiled by Francisco de Avila in Huarochirí (at the start of the 17th century), four ages of the gods are presented:

> In very ancient times there existed a *huaca* named Yananamca Tutañamca. After these *huacas*, there was another *huaca* by the name of Huallallo Carhuincho. This *huaca* was victorious. When he already had power, he ordered man to only have two children. One of these he devoured, the other, chosen by his parents out of love, he let live. And since then, when people died, they came back to life after five days, and in the same way, the fields matured five days after being sown. And these peoples, the peoples of this entire region, had many inhabitants. As these increased in number, and as they multiplied in this way, they lived miserably, even in the canyons and in the small flats in the canyons turned into *chacras*, digging and breaking the soil. They can even be seen to this day, in all parts, terrains that are sown,

both small and large. And in this time the birds were very beautiful, the *huritu* and the *caqui*, all yellow, or some of them red.

Some time afterwards, appeared another *huaca* that had the name Pariacaca. Thus, he threw out the people from all parts. Of the subsequent events and of Pariacaca himself, we will now talk. In that time, there existed a *huaca* named Cuniraya. He existed then. But we do not know well if Cuniraya was before or after Pariacaca, or if this Cuniraya existed at the same time and together with Viracocha, creator of man. Because the people who worshipped spoke thus: 'Cuniraya Viracocha, maker of man, maker of the world, you have everything it is possible to have. The chacras are yours. I, man, am yours.' And when they were to start some difficult task, they prayed to him, throwing coca leaves to the ground, saying, 'May this be remembered, that Cuniraya Viracocha foretells it.' And without seeing Viracocha, the ancients spoke of him and worshipped him. And furthermore, the master weavers who had a very difficult job, worshipped him and appealed to him.

In the first cases, the conflict between the divine and the other is visible ("this *huaca* was victorious"). Throughout the texts of Huarochirí, we can appreciate the different struggles of the gods, despite the fact that this account throws doubt on whether they coexisted or not or whether there was a "historical" sequence. What took place in the Andes, as well as in other parts of the world that are not a consequence of a "historical revelation" of God (as in the historic religions of Judaism, Christianity and Islam) is that a cyclical sequence does not signify the elimination of the "defeated" divinities in the battles of the gods that occur at the passing of one age to the next; these divinities remain even though their influence or "hiearchical" ranking varies in the sacred context. It is also worth pointing out that the final text of the quoted account, which refers to "the master weavers", is related directly to modern accounts that consider the universe as a fabric made by the divinity, in this case Wiraqocha.

The creation myths or ordering of the world, and the myths of the origin of the Incas allow us to move closer to their cosmovision. The celestial divinities fertilize the earth and then "go to the sky" or to "the ends of the world", or are converted into mountains (the summit of the "sacred mountain" has been referred to as "the closest sky"). The very mountains, their interiors, and the subsoil in general are considered in the Andes as the "place of production" of men and animals, both in ancient mythology as well as in contemporary oral traditions, since the earth (Pachamama), is always feminine, and the sky (Wiraqocha, Inti) is always masculine. The presence of first creators (Cámac, Pachaychachi, even Inka) is also acknowledged, and there are myths that signal that the "brothers" of Wiraqocha were sons of Cámac. Without doubt, there remains much to discuss because most of the information of the classic chronicles is based on the Cusco mythical cycle.

Calendar

The chronicles and contemporary ethnographic research have provided much information regarding the Andean calendar, with many different academic theories regarding the calendar and its organization, considering diverse, nominal variations corresponding to different regions of the Andes. In general terms, they deal with a calendar marked by solemn festivals identified with the months of the year and also strictly related to agriculture. Naturally, the most important festivities were related to the solstices: *Inti Raymi* (the "winter solstice" in June) and *Cápac Raymi* (the "summer solstice" in December). Different chroniclers have placed the start of the calendar at distinct moments but the safest theory is that it started in the month of December, corresponding to the summer solstice. The chronicler Juan de Betanzos, who lived and collected his information in Cusco, stated that Inca Yupanqui (Pachacuti) had ordered the organization of the calendar:

> And after this it set, when the sun set, in a certain place where it was safe to stand and from where it could be well seen, and thus from that site where it arose was known the course along which the sun went in a straight line in the highest of the mountains, he ordered built four pyramids or hewn marbles, the two in the middle smaller than the other two at the sides, and of two different heights each one, square and being one fathom apart, except for the two smaller ones which were closer together in the middle, being half a fathom one from the other. And when the sun came out, being there Inca Yupanqui stood up to look and size up this straight line, it comes out and goes straight to the middle of these two pillars. And when it set, the same for the part where it set. From this the common people understood the time that it was, thus to sow, as well as to harvest, because the clocks were four when the sun came out, and four again when it went down, from which the passing and moments that the sun thus made in the year were distinguished. Inca Yupanqui made a mistake in taking down the month so that they added one, and our count of the months of the year that he thus signalled, because they took December, when they should have taken January.

In this way, Betanzos highlighted that: a) The year began in December, although it differed from the western calendar; and b) It was set, in consequence, in line with the solstices and equinoxes. The following lists of months are those provided by Guamán Poma (ca. 1615) and in modern times by Valcárcel:

Guamán Poma		Valcárcel	
1	Cápac Raymi (January)	1	Cápac Raimi (December)
2	Paucar Uaray (February)	2	Uchuy Pocoy (January)
3	Pacha Pucuy (March)	3	Jatun Pocoy (February, fruits ripen)
4	Inca Raymi Quilla (April)	4	Páucar Huaray (March)
5	Aymoray Quilla (May, harvest)	5	Ayrihuay (April)
6	Cuzqui Quilla (June, Inti Raymi)	6	Aymuray (May, harvest)
7	Chacra Conacuy (July, distribution of terrains)	7	Inti Raimi (June, solar festival)
8	Chacra Yapui Quilla (August, sowing)	8	Anta Situha (July, purification)
9	Colla Raymi (September, lunar festival)	9	Cápac situha (August, great purification)
10	Uma Raymi Quilla (October, rain ceremony)	10	Uma Raymi (September, water festival)
11	Aymoray Quilla (November, dead)	11	Coya Raimi (October, festival of the *coya*)
12	Cápac Inti Raymi (December, great sun festival)	12	Aya Marca (November, dead)

The differences are visible although there is a certain correspondence, except for at the start of the year. Possibly, some of these variations originate with Guamán Poma employing information mainly coming from the central Andes, north of Cusco.

The Huacas and the Sacred

Huaca is a term that the chroniclers and the evangelizers used both to designate the "non-principal" gods (even though some extended it to cover all divinities) as well as the temples and other holy places. It is very possible that *huaca* would designate in generic terms everything that was holy. During the evangelization and the successive campaigns of extirpation of "idolatries", the Spaniards destroyed all *huaca* objects or figures that fell into their hands, but they were not able to destroy all the buildings and so, instead, they hung crosses on them, thus promoting syncretism.

It is a fact that *huaca* is a very wide term, that not just covers temples and other religious objects but also people and specific posts: The *curaca*s and the Inca were *huaca* and, as such, were not just able to communicate with the universe of the sacred but were also sacred themselves. For this reason, they were revered and *mochados* (offered a ritual salutation that consisted in an oral gesture, such as a kiss, and in the offering of eyelashes and eyebrows, as though it were a gesture) and there were also initiation rituals for each post, including of course the priests, who were often confused with the *curaca*s. The soothsayers, interpreters of divine decisions, formed an unquestioned part of the religious personnel , and they participated in distinct rituals not just related with the correct placement of the festivals or best occasions for sowing, harvesting, shearing and the rearing of livestock, but also with the rituals associated with rain, irrigation, the cleaning of canals and other favorable events, as well as in the initiation rituals of the *curaca*s, the members of the elite and the *Inca* himself.

The Inca Sun Religion

The chroniclers were in agreement in indicating the Sun (*Inti, Punchao*) as the most important and "official" Inca deity. They assigned to it, therefore, an exclusive status within the hierarchy, in such a way that some chroniclers suggested that there was a type of solar "evangelization", through which the official Inca religion was expanded and imposed on all the Andean populations. The latter case may be better understood as a projection of Christianity by the chroniclers as the Cusco sun religion was neither exclusive nor unique. The evangelizers of the 16th century concentrated their efforts of extirpation on the "idolatries" on the eradication of the Inca solar religion and on the destruction of popular cultural manifestations. This is due to the fact that they did not take into account other religious levels that entered more quickly into degrees of acculturation. A history of the evangelization that explores the widespread Andean syncretism remains to be written although there are many worthy studies of the subject.

In the chronicles of the Cusco cycle there may have been confusion regarding whether the Incas were descended from children of the sun or from Wiraqocha. However, the majority propose the former. As with the organization of the *Tawantinsuyu*, the solar religion reached preeminence and transformed into an official religion, according to the chroniclers, leaving the problem apparently resolved. I have previously proposed that the Sun (Inti, Punchao), being an ancient divinity in the Andes (*Willka* may have been one of its earlier names) replaced or displaced Wiraqocha in the mythical cycle that relates the war of Cusco with the Chancas, and the beginning of the great expansion of the *Tawantinsuyu*.

But at the same time, we should emphasize that the Cusco solar religion is not the only one, and that both the Hispanic documentation as well as contemporary ethnology have detailed the existence of other solar religions in the Andes, during and after the Incas. Although the chronicles stated that the Incas had imposed their principal god across the Andean region, their own evidence indicates that the Inca solar religion was elitist, and that it was in a good part restricted to the governing class of Cusco. The Incas built solar temples specifically in the administrative centers they organized in different places of their ample dominions; it has been said that each of these contained a "palace of the *Inca*", a solar temple and an Inca *aqllawasi* ("house of *aqllas*"). It should also be added that this would have included a complex of storehouses for the goods destined for redistribution, as well as the rooms and workshops of the *mittani* who worked there and who we previously have discussed. For this reason a chronicler such as Guamán Poma could identify the administrative centers as "other Cuscos". Speaking of these ordinances, which he attributed to Tupa Inca Yupanqui, Guamán Poma wrote that one of them stated: "And we order that there be another Cusco in Quito and another in Tumi [Tumi Pampa] and another in Guánuco [Guánuco Pampa] and another in Hatuncolla and another in the ponds and calash that is Cusco ..." Other data provided by different chroniclers allows us to appreciate that during the campaigns of conquest, for example, a "replica" of Cusco, that would fit in the "other Cuscos" of Guamán Poma, was built in Huarco, near Cañete, on the central coast of Peru. Other places, such as Vilcas Guamán or Cajamarca, were administrative centers of the same type. In each of these centers there were therefore Cusco solar temples, served by priests linked to the Cusco elite.

The most important sun temple was found in Cusco and is referred to as *Coricancha* in most of the chronicles. There are abundant extracts in these works that describe it and one chronicler even provided an account in which he described it as the "main temple". There is no evidence in the chronicles that anyone from outside the Cusco elite entered Coricancha, and it is even mentioned that in some parts of this maximum temple only the *Inca* could enter. But there were other temples that generally were linked to the solar religion; these were the *ushnu*, pyramids placed on esplanades and in which various apparently solar rituals were undertaken, and the first of these was found in Aucaypata, one of the parts of the great central square of the city of Cusco (the other part was called Cusipata). The chronicles mention mass ceremonies in the great square of Cusco, and it is stated that the *curaca*s attended these, including even those from the furthest regions, participating in specific sun festivals. It appears that the participation of the general population in the Inca sun religion was limited to specific ceremonies in the *ushnu*, but there is no evidence that there was any type of direct participation. Nor do we find a proliferation of solar temples that would make us think that there was a generalized presence of the population in the Inca religion.

The priests of the official religion, whatever their rank, were likewise associated with the ruling class of Cusco. The maximum authority was called *Willaq Umu* (the chronicles gave him various names including *Vilahoma*), a figure whose importance and prestige was appreciated at first hand by the first Spaniards, since they saw him act in the moments prior to the invasion, especially during the first Andean rebellion against the Spaniards, that was directed by members of the Cusco elite and was led by Manco Inca, son of Huayna Cápac, in 1536. In a similar fashion, the chronicles present a series of types of priest, which vary naturally from region to region. Recent research has highlighted again the priest-role of the Andean *curacas*, and this can be especially appreciated in the processes of extirpation of idolatries following the Spanish invasion.

Chapter VII
Art and Culture

In talking about Inca art, the majority of authors tend to contrast the art prior to the *Tawantinsuyu* with that which spread during the Inca Empire. This contrast is rooted in particular in the richness and multiplicity of the artistic expressions that predate the Incas and the loss of creativity that appeared to occur during Cusco's domination. It is certain that this claim is principally based on the ceramics that some societies predating the Incas developed to extraordinary levels. However, it can also be argued that, in general terms, Inca culture reached unprecedented levels in the diffusion of its styles, and that this was connected without doubt to the way in which the Incas made certain Andean styles their own, taking this to an extreme of generalization. This was nothing other than the mass production and use of ceramic styles, and the standardization of textiles, and this responded evidently to the fact that the *Tawantinsuyu* organized a regime that made possible the existence of a supra-ethnic or "state circuit" for the circulation of goods, namely the redistribution exercised by the *Inca*.

The chroniclers of the 16th and 17th centuries gave amazing testimony regarding Andean architecture. We could quote whole pages from their commentaries; just as occurred in other lands, they were however unable to distinguish between that which had been constructed by the Incas and that of their predecessors in the Andes. The chronicles frequently highlighted the grandiosity of the buildings, the amazing stonemasonry and the almost incredible armor and assembly of the stone panels in the walls. They also spoke of the great cities and pyramids of adobe, although generally they preferred the stone constructions. Likewise they highlighted the cities, fortresses, palaces and temples, agricultural terraces, and irrigation canals, and they emphasized the roads, continuously comparing them to the great Roman roads. They also stressed the absence of iron in the tools, but at the same time they called attention to the ingenuity that made possible these great buildings that they described. Thus, for example, P. Bernabé Cobo detailed their method of moving the stones, many of which were of great dimensions:

> They brought them [the stones] to where they were needed, dragging them. And as they lacked wheels and the wit to raise them, they made a steep escarpment next to the work, and by rolling them they moved them up. And as the building grew, they raised the escarpment. This method I saw used in the cathedral of Cusco which is being built.

It is already sufficiently well known that the Incas reproduced and renewed many earlier urban styles. In construction, both in "cities" or administrative centers and in concrete structures, the Incas borrowed elements that had been developed before them in the Andes, especially during the Middle Horizon. What also characterized the Incas here is their undoubted capacity for standardizing certain elements, bringing them to a mass level by opening up their uses in new parts of the Andes. Many of the urban nuclei of the Incas were built on previous settlements, as occurred with Cajamarca, or incorporated other elements in nuclei that already existed, as happened in the extensive "ceremonial city" of Pachacámac, located south of Lima. They extended their routes and constructions into zones very distant from the central area of their empire, such as the northeast of Argentine and the lands of present day Ecuador. Undoubtedly a large part of their settlements, especially along the edges of the central Andes, were realized with the purpose of colonization and defense, but in the construction that took place right up until the last days of the *Tawantinsuyu* we can also appreciate that the Spanish invasion of the 16th century occupied a still growing political space.

Modern authors (Gasparini and Margolies, for example) highlight the architecture of power, which better qualifies most Inca architecture than the more ancient authors' descriptions of this monumental culture. The architecture of power refers to those constructions destined for collective or "mass" purposes which were separated or differentiated from others with more limited uses, as occurred with some temples, which were basically for the use of the elite, such as Coricancha, although the *inkawasi* or "palaces of the Inka" and the *aqllawasi* are also mentioned among these restricted buildings. It is true that much can be debated regarding the use of certain constructions or complexes, known since the chronicles as "fortresses" or *huacas*.

One kind of construction constantly repeated across the *Tawantinsuyu* is what the Spaniards referred to as "sheds" (a fortuitous Americanism), great constructions with gabled roofs, highlighted in various places by the chroniclers since their first days in the Andes. Some appear in Cusco's central square, in which, as Inca Garcilaso de la Vega relates, the "royal houses" found around the square were or incorporated "sheds"; his text allows room for doubt. The largest of them was called *Cassana*, "was capable of holding 3,000 people" and was supposed to have been built by Pachacuti. Garcilaso adds: "...[it was]an incredible thing that there could be timber capable of covering such great pieces". These sheds, which the chroniclers described many times, were called *kallanka*, and the *Vocabulary*, by Diego González Holguín, notes: "*Callanca-rumi*. Large worked stones, a set of seats for foundations and thresholds. *Callanca huaci.* House founded upon these". The term indicates, therefore, a type of construction with foundations or a "base" of worked stones. The reference to the base is precise, and the upper part of the walls could easily be adobe.

These buildings had different functions, and archaeologists note their presence in practically all urban centers and Inca nuclei. They were sometimes identifiable with buildings that were traditionally called temples, such as occurred with the classical building of Cacha or Raqchi (see photo 4), which the traditional accounts gathered by the chroniclers attributed to the god Wiraqhocha, whose temple it was. The chronicles indicated that after the defeat of the Chancas, Pachacuti (or Wiraqocha in one text), the victor in the contest, ordered it built. Garcilaso de Vega described it, as did Cieza de León. It was a great construction more than 90 meters in length and 25 meters wide, with solid foundations of stone and walls of adobe, with two rows of round columns and a kind of short central wall running lengthways. Garcilaso stated that the Inca ordered that

> [...]the form of the temple should imitate, as much as was possible, the place where [the divinity] appeared; it should be [like the field] uncovered, without a roof; that a small chapel be made, covered with stone, which looks like the hollow in the rock where he was lying down, that had a *sobrado*, above the ground...

Sobrado is a kind of garret. Garcilaso also added that it this kind of construction was not customary and continued:

> The door that looked eastwards served as the entrance and exit of the temple. It was in the middle of the gable and because those Indians did not know how to make vaults in order to make attics above, they made walls of the same piece of stone, which served as rafters, because they lasted more than if they were of wood. They placed them at a

distance, leaving a gap of seven feet between wall and wall, and the walls were three feet solid and there were 12 narrow alleys formed by these walls. They shut these off from above, instead of boards, with slabs of stone 10 feet long and half a staff high [...].

These last phrases tend to leave the impression of an attic that was in reality a second floor. However, contemporary research has ruled out this theory and, as Gasparini and Margolies thought, it is probable that Garcilaso's description was not a first-hand account but rather that of a third party (photo 4 shows the actual remains as well as the idealized reconstruction that these two authors undertook, which appears closer to the reality). It was always said that the Incas did not build with round columns although this building is a known exception.

Photo 4. Raqchi.

Mariana Mould de Pease

Coricancha is the most famous temple in the chronicles. Dedicated to the sun (Inti), it has been described as having walls covered with gold leaf and other sumptuous adornments. It is also reputed to have had a garden of gold where all the important plants of the Andean area were represented, starting with maize, the solar plant *par excellence*. Myth and legend surround Coricancha, built, according to the chroniclers by Manco Cápac, the first *Inca* according to Andean oral tradition, and subsequently modified by two *Incas* who have special significance in the chronicles, Pachacuti and Huayna Cápac. Built in front of the square of Intipampa, it was without any doubt the most important religious center in Inca Cusco, and from it radiated the *ceques* that linked the many places of worship that existed in Cusco. The descriptions of the chroniclers highlighted the particular evidence of the beautiful stonemasonry of their walls, part of which remain to this day, up to the point that one of the best known authors of the 16th century, Pedro Cieza de León, boasted about it, saying that he had never known anything similar except the "tower that I saw in Toledo when I went to present the First Part of my chronicle to Prince Phillip, which is the hospital that Tavera, the Archbishop of Toledo, ordered built".

Cieza de León highlighted the stone, which was both noteworthy because of its natural form as well as the masonry realized with it. He calls attention to the existence of "a belt of gold two palms wide and four fingers from the altar" in the middle of the wall of Coricancha and notes that the façade and doors were "plated" with this metal. He likewise describes the interiors of the temple, particularly indicating that in one of the rooms "there was the figure of the son, very large, made of gold, worked very primitively, mounted with many fine stones. There was in that [room] some packages [mummies] of the deceased *Incas* who had reigned in Cusco, with a great multitude of treasures".

In general terms, the authors who studied Inca architecture highlighted the monumentality of their constructions even though some mentioned a "megalithic era" prior to the Incas, characterized by those great constructions that, like Tiawanacu and Sacsaywaman, supported the theories about lost civilizations, including those populated by giants, a common theme among the authors of the 16th and 17th centuries that lasted until the beginning of modern anthropology.

Regarding ceramics, the aesthetic contrast between Andean societies prior to the Incas and the Incas themselves has been highlighted, with the artistic quality of the latter considered clearly inferior. The types classically identified as examples of Inca ceramics are the so-called *aríbalos*, named thus in recollection of the Greek amphorae of that name. They reached up to 1.5 meters in height and had various symbolic decorations, many of them geometric. They used lateral handles, with a protuberance generally representing the head of an animal. Both the handles and the animal head allowed them to be transported on the shoulders, tied down with a belt or cord as they were used to carry *chicha* or water (see photo 5). Certainly, there were more forms employed in Inca ceramics than that of the *aríbalo*, and there were many with the *kero* also standing out. This was a form of vase although generally the most mentioned are made of wood and decorated pictorially.

The most interesting thing about Inca ceramics is its notable mass production, both in terms of the standardization achieved in the decorative styles and inspirations as well as the organization of this production on a great scale. In the text reproduced (Chapter IV) regarding the human energy that the Chupchay ethnic group provided to the *Tawantinsuyu*, there figure "40 potters to make pots and they took these to Guánuco". But the *Tawantinsuyu* also organized ways of working ceramic on a larger scale, as can be appreciated among

Photo N° 5. Aríbalo.
(Museo Inka, Cusco)

Joge Flores Ochoa

the Lupaqa of Lake Titicaca. There the Incas established a town with an apparent predominance of potters, in Cupi, in the present day zone of Huancané, where people from the Lupaqa and neighboring ethnic groups were concentrated in a total of around 1,000 families, although not all were dedicated to the production of ceramics, and possibly it was a similar productive center, albeit on a lesser scale, to the larger complex of Huánuco Pampa.

Much has been written regarding weaving in the Andes, highlighting especially not just its economic significance but also its ritual meaning. It is worthwhile repeating here that during the journeys of the *Inca* around the Andes, he distributed clothing in the form of redistribution. In the mythical accounts of Huarochirí, in the central sierra of Peru, it is also reported that the master weavers principally worshipped Wiraqocha, and we can therefore construct

Photo N° 6.
Huánuco Pampa

Luis Barreda Murillo

Mariana Mould de Pease

Photo N° 7. Machu Picchu

155

an image of this divinity as a weaver and that of the universe as a weaving. We can also state the same regarding the advent of mass production of weaving in the times of the Incas as we did for ceramics, as well as contrasting it with the extraordinary artistic quality of the weaving produced by prior peoples. It is also worth highlighting that, again like in the case of ceramics, this mass production and use did not entail a drop in technological standards. But certainly beyond the great volumes of textiles produced under the *mitta* regime and kept in the storehouses, the Cusco administration introduced this weaving into many parts of the Andes, and maintained the quality and symbolic value of cloth, especially regarding the gifts of the *Inca*. Weavings thus had an intense ritual value as they formed part of the offerings to the divinities and also the funerary paraphernalia.

The Incas used textiles for redistribution, especially wool, although they also used cotton. There are specific testimonies, such as the list mentioned in Chapter IV, which provides a good example of the way individuals were assigned to weave. Andean textiles were, in the 16th century, basically of two types (although there had previously always been more); *abasca* and *cumbi*. The latter was more appreciated for ritual uses, bordered with great quality and made on special looms. The chroniclers highlight the softness of *cumbi* and even compare it with the finest European cloth at the time, sometimes arguing that the Andean product was best. It is also very possible that the production of *cumbi* was itself surrounded by a ritual context. *Abasca* was a homemade product, less specialized and, certainly, more widespread. P. Bernabé Cobo, who finished writing his *History of the New World* around 1653, noted the existence of up to five different types of textiles during the Inca period:

> They made five distinctions in ancient times in cloth and weavings of wool: One coarse and thick, that they call *abasca*; another very fine and precious, called *cumbi*; the third was of colored feathers woven

together and laid over *cumbi*; the fourth was a fabric of silver and was bordered with *chaquira*; and the fifth was a very thick, coarse material that served as carpet and blanket. The cloth of *abasca* they weaved from the coarser wool of llamas or rams of the earth [*sic*. This appears to be a reference to vicuñas.] and the plebian people wore this. They worked almost all of it with the color of the wool itself, although they also had cotton. That of *cumbi*, of the finer, selected wool, and the most delicate and precious *cumbis* of the wool of lambs, which is very delicate. They made some so thin and lustrous as *gorborán*, and they gave it the same colors as cotton. The kings, great lords and all the nobility of the kingdom wore these clothes, and the common people could not use it. The *Inca* had in many places very senior officials, known as *cumbicamayos*, who did not engage in anything but weaving and working cumbis. These were ordinary men, although the *mamaconas* also used to weave them and those that came from their hands were the finest and most delicate.

Regarding metallurgy, the most important achievement of the Incas was the dissemination of the production of bronze, which the chroniclers mention and the archaeologists of today have revealed, calling attention to the fact that during the *Tawantinsuyu*, bronze was a disposable material given the volume of it produced. The Incas did not better the prized work of the inhabitants of Chimor (on the northern coast) in silver and gold, and the achievements of the latter with precious metals is well known. However, we should also take into account that the sacking of Cusco was so sustained and the search for hidden treasures so greedy. At the same time, we should be aware that, after the conquest of Chimor by the Incas, many specialists from that region were transferred to other areas as *mitmaqkuna* of the *Inca*.

Chapter VIII
The Incas after the Spanish Invasion

The *Inca* Atahualpa was captured by Francisco Pizarro in Cajamarca. The Spaniards entered this city on November 15th, 1532. They came from a long journey begun in Panama years earlier, and they had travelled the waters of the Pacific in repeated journeys. They had been in the Ecuadorian rainforests west of the Andes and they had barely overcome the ravages of the climate and the hostility of tropical diseases. They had first come across the subjects of the *Inca* when they found a raft off the Peruvian coast, and afterwards they had established clearer contacts when they occupied the island of Puna and disembarked in Tumbes. They then founded San Miguel de Piura. From there they headed to Cajamarca.

The chronicles describe with abundant details the first moments of the occupation of the Andes, providing the particulars of the events of Cajamarca, where the *Inca* entered in a long ceremonial procession cut short by Friar Vicente Valverde, who is said to have begun a conversation with the Inca and notified him of the *requerimiento* as there was a royal provision that this text, which contained a demand to submit before the Spanish crown and Christianity, be read. Atahualpa listened to it, almost certainly through a terrible translation, and appears to have been intrigued with the breviary that the friar had, and was thus given it. On being unable to understand its use, the *Inca* threw it to the ground. This appears to have unleashed the Spanish aggression, the fruit of which was many deaths and the capture of the *Inca* himself. Once a prisoner, Atahualpa agreed a ransom and huge quantities of gold and silver from all corners of the *Tawantinsuyu* arrived in Cajamaraca. Despite this, and using as a pretext the defiance of the *Inca*, the Spaniards executed him on July 26th, 1533. Their justification for execution was supported by the news that, as a prisoner, Atahualpa had ordered the killing of Huáscar, his rival in the war that began on the death of the previous *Inca*, Huana Cápac. At the time, Huáscar was prisoner of the troops of Atahualpa, and the Spaniards understood him to be the "legitimate heir" whereas Atahualpa was presented by the chroniclers as an "usurper and bastard"; as a result, his death hastened Huáscar's right to the Inca throne.

With the *Inca* dead, Pizarro advanced towards the south, towards Cusco, the city that had been acclaimed since the first moments of the Spanish invasion, to such a degree that some of the first chroniclers did not hesitate to refer to the *Inca* as "Cusco". During their trip, Tupa Huallpa, who the chroniclers often called *Toparpa* or even *Atahualpa*, was declared the successor to Atahualpa. He was the son of Huayna Cápac and died on the journey to Cusco, presumably poisoned. After many vagaries, Francisco Pizarro and his band entered Cusco on November 14th, 1533. A little earlier, the chronicles mention, a meeting between Pizarro and Manco Inca, another son of Huayna Cápac, who was recognized by the Spaniards as the "heir to the throne". The chroniclers give meticulous accounts of this journey of conquest, noting that the Spaniards were continually threatened by Inca troops loyal to Aahualpa, and they presented the Spaniards as favorable to the faction of Huáscar and his "party" since, as mentioned earlier, they considered him the legitimate heir to Huayna Cápac. The chronicles likewise state that Cusco had been sacked by the troops of Atahualpa and the harmony between the people of Cusco and the invaders was thanks to this event, they explain. However, this harmony does not appear to be the whole story.

In any case, the peace lasted a short time. Manco Inca and the people of Cusco were witnesses to an uncontrolled search for riches that marked the early days of the Spaniards in the Andes. The chronicles related amazing stories of the zealous search for treasures and the legend rapidly grew that many treasures had been buried by the Incas. These accounts even passed into Andean mythology compiled in our times.

Initially, Manco Inca collaborated with the Spaniards in their struggle with the troops loyal to Atahualpa, commanded by Quisquis, who was defeated but not taken prisoner. But the demands of the Spaniards appear to have exceeded any possibility of harmony and Manco Inca attempted to leave Cusco in 1535 while Francisco Pizarro was in Lima. He was found and obliged to return to the city. On attempting to flee again, he was imprisoned. While this was happening, Pizarro's partner, Diego de Almagro, had headed off to conquer Chile. With him went Huillac Umu, the Inca high priest. After being badly treated, in the middle of their march, he returned to Cusco. On his return, the uprising was hatched. The chroniclers write that Manco Inco humored Hernando Pizarro's greed by offering him treasures, and was thus left free. Manco Inca was thus able to leave the city and launch his rebellion against the Spaniards in May 1536.

Manco Inca's siege of Cusco gave rise to an epic related by the chroniclers in which prodigious feats of bravery and miraculous apparitions of the Virgin Mary as well as the Apostle James battling above the clouds on his white horse and helping the Christians against the *Infidels*, a term commonly used in the chronicles to refer to Andean peoples. Cusco was set alight, with much of the city destroyed other than the buildings surrounding Aucaypata square. There the Spaniards took refuge, attributing their salvation to the help of the Virgin

Mary, who protected their refuge from the flames. Afterwards, the Church of the Triumph was built on this spot, next to the cathedral. Manco Inca's troops arrived to take control of Sacsaywaman, but were forced out afterwards. Between May and July, the city was in a grim situation. Finally, the siege was lifted, apparently as a result of a shortage of supplies for the besiegers. At almost the same time as Cusco was under siege, the recently founded city of Lima was suffering a similar fate, and the Spaniards lived difficult days. They survived these and Francisco Pizarro organized an expedition to help the Spaniards in Cusco, carrying out a campaign of repression in his journey through the central mountains of Peru.

Manco Inca fled with some of his troops, taking refuge in a mountainous region identified by the generic name Vilcabamba. From there he waged a long war against the Spaniards, continued by his successors, and which only concluded in 1571 when the troops of the Viceroy Francisco de Toledo entered the area and eliminated this focus of Inca resistance. Around 1541, Manco Inca managed to rescue his son Titu Cusi Yupanqui, who had remained in Cusco. A little later, several Spaniards aligned with Diego de Almagro, who had been defeated in the war with Pizarro, arrived in Vilcabamba, befriending Manco Inca and living there under his protection. Sometime in early 1545, as a result of a gaming dispute, they killed Manco Inca and were themselves then executed by his supporters. On Manco Inca's death, one of his sons, Sayri Tupa, took his place and, 12 years later, signed a treaty of surrender with the Viceroy Marquess of Cañete, and subsequently moved to Cusco. Meanwhile, his brother, Titu Cusi Yapanqui, continued his resistance in Vilcabamba and was then succeeded by Tupa Amaro, who was finally taken prisoner by troops of the Viceroy Francisco de Toledo and executed in Cusco in 1572.

The *Incas* of Vilcabamba were one of the initial forms of Andean resistance. Another was the struggle undertaken by the generals of

Atahualpa, especially Quisquis and Rumiñahi, as well as Calcuchima, even though he was taken prisoner and executed by the Spaniards. The *Incas* of Vilcabamba placed constant pressure on the nascent Spanish colony, drawing a battle line between Cusco and Lima, which was constantly subject to attacks until 1571. But the Incas of Vilcabamba also provided another type of pressure that caused problems for the Spanish administration in the Andes, given that the survival of Vilcabamba must have provided a source of cohesion for the population, especially in the early days. However, the subject is not that simple since not all members of the Cusco elite were able to live alongside Manco Inca and a section of them remained in Cusco; this group was strengthened when its numbers were swelled as Sayri Tupca reached agreement with the Spanish crown in 1588. The survivors of the Cusco elite in the 16th century had, nevertheless, an eventful existence, interwoven with the internal conflicts of the ruling group that had been defeated in the Spanish invasion.

It is inarguable that Manco Inca exercised effective leadership in the times of his uprising and even after it, but it is not clearly established what was the real achievement of the *Incas* of Vilcabamba in the first 40 years of colonial life, in particular after the murder of Manco Inca, given that his presence brought recognition for the group (although in reality this fact is much less documented than other aspects of Hispanic history of these years) and on the other hand, it is reported that they supported and organized the Andean resistance against the Spanish colonization throughout the period from 1535-1536 to 1572, the year in which the final leader of Vilcabamba, Tupa Amaru, was executed in Cusco.

This resistance was comprised specifically of the subversive actions of Andean movements that have been qualified as *nativist* or messianic, that rose up in rural areas around 1565 and that were repressed by the Spanish viceroy. The best known of these movements was the

Taqui Onqoy, although there are also references to others of the same era and with similar characteristics, such as the Moro Onqoy and Yanahuara. As is natural, almost the only references that we now have regarding these resistance activities come from the Spanish reports of the era, which inevitably tend to lay responsibility with the *Incas* of Vilcabamba for all subversive activity of that era. It is more probable, however, that these movements of the 16th century correspond more to the resistance activities of the *curacas*, whose authority recovered independence notably as a result of the collapse of the *Tawantinsuyu* and the populations most connected to Inca Cusco. The Spanish account regarding Manco Inca is equally marked by the events of Spanish politics and the conflicts that existed between the Spaniards in the Andes at that time. A good example is the fact that Manco Inca received in Vilcabamba sympathizers of Diego de Almagro, who ended up killing him. Some time afterwards, when the envoy of the Crown, Cristóbal Vaca de Castro defeated "the boy" Diego de Almagro, (the son of Francisco Pizarro's associate) in the Battle of Chupas, it turned out that the defeated leader wanted to take refuge in Vilcabamba. There are, then, indicators of certain links between the *Almagristas* and the Inca resistance.

If the resistance activities in the Andes of the 16th century are not directly and uniquely attributable to the *Incas* of Vilcabamba, they are to the ethnic groups and the *curacas*. The Andean *curacas* started in the 16th century a varied range of activities that went from subversion to adapting to the Spanish system, the latter of which did not exclude the former as we have evidence of the *curacas* presenting resources to the Spanish crown in order to validate their political status while at the same time organizing uprisings and actively participating in them.

Part of the Cusco elite remained in the Spanish city and did not go to Vilcabamba with Manco Inca. However, it has been thought that there existed links with the resistance group in Vilcabamba. The most notable person of the Inca elite of Cusco in the 16th century is Paullu, who is frequently mentioned as an ally of the Spaniards, with whom he collaborated closely. It is not clear if Paullu Inca sought to help the Spanish in order to receive equivalent support that would allow him to assume effective leadership among the Cusco elite. It should also be taken into consideration that the titles of Manco Inca came from the Spaniards, who assumed that the simple fact of being the "legitimate" son of Huayna Cápac gave him the right to automatically become *Inca*. The chroniclers distinguished various moments in the attitudes of Paullu, relating him without doubt to the gradual *rapprochement* with Christianity and final acceptance of baptism. For this very reason, the Spaniards recognized him as the most obvious leader of the Cusco Inca group. The attitude of the Andean people was distinct, since although there is no testimony that Manco Inca had been initiated as *Inca*, it is notable that he was able to bring together the resistance of an important part of the Incas. He did not do the same thing with the general population and his role in the movements previously mentioned was marginal at best. The *Inca* does not appear among the principal personalities of the Taqui Onqoy or other activities of the Andean resistance in the 16th century. However, the Andean *huacas* do figure massively and the leaders of the most studied movements acted in their name and not that of the *Inca*.

The loss of Andean prestige of the Vilcabamba *Incas* was not related to an abstract political scheme but specifically to the breakdown of the redistribution that the *Inca* exercised. In previous chapters, especially that dedicated to the economy, we have noted how the political power of the *Inca* was structured upon the base of redistribution that he organized. It was not, therefore, an abstract political entity that provided the foundations for his prestige and that made his power viable. Nor was it pure and simple domination, but rather the complex system of relationships generated around and through redistribution. As a result of the collapse of the *Tawantinsuyu*, the ethnic groups saw the chain of redistribution broken, and although they tried to establish it with the Spaniards, they were unsuccessful; for this reason the relationship between the *Incas* of Vilcabamba and the Andean ethnic groups should be viewed as weaker in line with the diminishing possibilities of restructuring redistribution relationships. Although we have mentioned the relationships of the Vilcabamba *Incas* with some ethnic groups, we do not understand the process of the crisis of redistribution. However, it was natural that the Spaniards of the 16th century attributed to the leadership of Vilcabamba the organizing of all subversive activities, given that they believed the Inca political structure to be similar to that existing in European kingdoms.

In the 16th century, the survivors of the Cusco elite appear to have established a similar relationship with the Spanish crown to that of the *curaca*s of diverse Andean zones; they sought to have their privileges as "nobles" (understood in the European sense) recognized without this precluding their participation in multiple uprisings and specifically in the resistance headed by Manco Inca. In the same manner, the Andean *curaca*s provided much proof of their loyal services to the Spanish crown and at the same time participated in multiple rebellions throughout the colonial process. It is very probable that the leadership capacity of the Cusco elite was affected by its drastic diminution, which may have begun before the Spanish invasion, since the chronicles mentioned that one of the consequences of the triumph of Atahualpa over Huáscar was the destruction of a considerable sector of the Cusco leadership. It must also have seen its numbers reduced as a result of the Spanish invasion and as a consequence of the resistance itself, as well as the wars among the Spaniards, who used the Cusco leaders to organize the support of various sectors of the population. All this reduced without doubt the political capacity of the elite as it was progressively disconnected from the Andean population, due to Spanish control, its decrease in numbers and its inability to reestablish the redistribution that had sustained its previous power.

We know little, in truth, about the activities of the Cusco elite in the 17th century, and the diminution in their power is usually accepted given the deterioration experienced in the previous century by the descendants of the Cusco *panaqa*. There is evidence that they continued their conduct aimed at the consolidation of privileges under the new regime, but not regarding whether they intervened in uprisings after Manco Inca. Only in the 16th century can we find their presence in Andean uprisings, outside of Cusco and documented in just a few cases, just as the figure of the *Inca* reappears with messianic colorings. But it is in the 18th century, at the same time as the leaders of the Cusco *panaqa* reappear surrounded by an aura of rebirth, appreciable in the famous portraits that they ordered painted in that time, and in which they appear dressed in their traditional robes, the *Inca* is clearly a messianic hero who feeds into the anti-Spanish movements of the era, and Cusco's prestige is presented as unquestioned. At the same time, there was an increase in the number of administrative proceedings in which the descendants of the *Incas* sought (Hispanic) legal recognition. The most famous of these was that undertaken by José Gabriel Tupa Amaro, the leader of the greatest and best known Andean rebellion, at the end of the 18th century. In that same century, there were many other movements or uprisings against the Spanish crown and its domination of the Andes. In all of these, the presence of the resurrected *Inca* is an element of the greatest importance. The Spaniards left abundant testimonies of this, and the theme has received great attention in recent years.

It is notable that there was a change in attitude of the Cusco leadership in the 18th century related to two important situations mentioned previously: a) The rise in the image of the *Inca* presented as a messianic hero among the general Andean population, a fact visible since the previous century; and b) The fact that the elite again developed an awareness of itself as leaders, a tendency fed in various ways, including, for example, the spread of several works that exalted the glorious past of the Incas, such as the case of the *Royal Commentaries of the Incas* by Inca Garcilaso de la Vega, reprinted in Spain in 1723-1724 and which circulated among the descendants of the old Cusco elite. José Gabriel Tupa Amaru actually acquired copies of this work and, after his rebellion, the Spanish crown, effectively prohibited the circulation of this book and ordered the requisition of all copies.

During the Colony, an image of the *glorious past* was thus generated, exemplified in the Incas of Cusco. The Andean population administered this image in its own way, not necessarily with the historical categories that the Spaniards used to explain it. In recent years, as the search intensified for a vision of Peruvian history that included and considered Andean perspectives, we have come to better understand the significance of Andean representations of the past, as well as their mythical and ritual expression.

There remains much to be discovered regarding the history of the Incas. However, their role in the formation of what today is Peru is beyond debate. This does not just refer to the configuration of a splendid past but also in particular the recognition of the capacity of humans in the Andes to organize an effective form of life. The most recent research attempts to get closer to the activity of Andean man during the Colony and the Republic, as well as the form in which he represented his own experience in new and different times. We will thus better understand the creative activity of the population. This understanding is important for the history of Peru then and now.

Glossary of Quechua terms

AYLLU
: Various meanings but principally used to denote community, clan or extended family.

CEQUE
: Alignment or line ordering the universe. In the Inca cosmovision, a complex system of *ceques* radiated out from Cusco.

CURACA
: Clan chief or supreme official.

HUACA
: Can be used as both a noun and adjective to mean either divine or sacred, or divinity. Often used specifically to denote a holy place such as a burial mound or shrine.

HANAN
: Denotes the upper half of the Andean duality. Can refer to physical or metaphysical qualities; for example, mountains, daytme, man and the Sun are all *hanan*.

INCA
: In addition to the people of the Inca Empire, this term denotes the supreme ruler of the Empire. As referenced in the text, scholars continue to debate the status of the Inca and, in particular, whether there may have been more than one at any point in time.

KHIPU
A cord used for accounting purposes, with knots and colored strands indicating quantities and other information. Some scholars now believe that *khipus* may have contained more complex information than statistical data and may even be equivalent to a primitive form of writing.

MITA
A compulsory unit of labor dedicated to the public good or the benefit of the *Tawantinsuyu* and that could range from a dayshift to an entire season.

PANAQA
A royal or aristocratic *ayllu*.

QOLLQA
A storehouse or granary.

TAWANTINSUYU
The Inca Empire, which was comprised of four parts or *suyu,* and is often translated as "The four quarters of the world".

URIN
The lower half of the Andean duality. Things which the Incas viewed as *urin* included women, the coast, the rainforest, water and night.

Basic Bibliography

ALBERTI, Giorgio & Enrique MAYER (eds.) (1974). *Reciprocidad e intercambio en los Andes peruanos*. Lima: Instituto de Estudios Peruanos.

CASTELLI, Amalia, Marcia KOTH DE PAREDES & Mariana MOULD DE PEASE (editores) (1981). *Etnohistoria y Antropología Andina*. Lima: Museo Nacional de Historia

CUNOW, Heinrich (1929). *El sistema de parentesco peruano y las comunidades gentilicias de los Incas*. Lima: Imp. de Le Livre.

CUNOW, Heinrich (1933). *La organización social del imperio de los Incas*. Lima: Librería y Editorial Peruana de Domingo Miranda.

DUVIOLS, Pierre (1971). *La lutte de las religions autochtones dans le Pèrou colonial. L´extirpation de l´idolatrie entre 1532 et 1600*. Paris: Institut Français d'Etudes Andines.

DUVIOLS, Pierre (1980). Algunas reflexiones acerca de las tesis de la estructura dual del poder incaico. *Historica* IV, 2, Lima.

FLORES OCHOA, Jorge (1976). Enqa, enqaychu, illa y khuya runi. Aspectos mágico-religiosos entre pastores. *Journal de la Societé des Americanistes*. LXIII, Lima.

GASPARINI, Graciano & Luise MARGOLIES (1977). *Arquitectura inka*. Caracas: Centro de Investigaciones Históricas y Estéticas. Universidad Central de Venezuela.

KOTH DE PAREDES, Marcia & Amalia CASTELLI (eds.) (1979). *Etnohistoria y Antropología Andina*. Lima: Fulbright Comission.

MEANS, Philip Ainsworth (1928). *Biblioteca Andina*. Translations of the Conneticut Academy of Arts and Sciences, 28, New Haven.

MORRIS, Craig (1973). Establecimientos estatales en el Tawantinsuyu: una estrategia de urbanismo obligado. *Revista del Museo Nacional* XXXIX, Lima.

MURRA, John V. (1975). *Formaciones económicas y políticas del mundo andino*. Lima: Instituto de Estudios Peruanos.

MURRA, John V. (1978). *La organización económica del Estado Inca*. México: Siglo XXI.

MURRA, John V. (1980). Derechos a las tierras en el Tawantinsuyo. *Revista de la Universidad Complutense*. XXVIII, 117, Madrid.

MURRA, John V. (1983). La Mit'a al Tawantinsuyo: prestaciones de los grupos étnicos. *Chungura*, 10, Arica.

MURRA, John V. (1987). ¿Existieron el tributo y los mercados antes de la invasión europea? In Harris, Olivias, Brooke, Larson & Tandeter (eds.), *La participación indígena en los mercados surandinos. Estrategias y reproducción social. Siglos XVI a XX*. La Paz: CERES.

ORTIZ RESCANIERE, Alejandro (1973). *De Adaneva a Inkarri. Una visión indígena del Perú*. Lima: Retablo de Papel Ediciones.

OSSIO, JUAN M. (editor) (1973). *Ideología mesiánica del mundo andino*. Lima: Ignacio Prado Pastor.

PEASE G.Y., Franklin (1973). *El dios creador andino*. Lima: Mosca Azul.

PEASE G.Y., Franklin (1986). La noción de propiedad entre los Incas: una aproximación. In Shozo Matsuda (ed.), *Etnografía e historia del mundo andino: continuidad y cambio*. Tokio: University of Tokio.

PEASE G.Y., Franklin (1989). *Del Tawantinsuyu a la historia del Perú*. Second Edition. Lima: Fondo Editorial PUCP.

PEASE G.Y., Franklin (1990a) Ritual y conquista incaica. *Boletín del Instituto Riva Agüero* 16, Lima.

PEASE G.Y., Franklin (1990b) *Inca y kuraka, Relaciones de poder y representación histórica.* Maryland: University of Maryland, College Park.

PEASE G.Y., Franklin (1991). *Los últimos Incas del Cuzco.* Madrid: Alianza Editorial.

PEASE G.Y., Franklin (editor) (1977). *Collaguas I.* Lima: Fondo Editorial PUCP.

PEASE G.Y., Franklin (1982). *El pensamiento mítico.* Anthology. Lima: Mosca Azul.

PLATT, Tristan (1980). Espejos y maíz: el concepto de yanatin entre los Macha de Bolivia. En Mayer y Bolton (editores). *Parentesco y matrimonio en los Andes.* Lima: Fondo Editorial PUCP.

PORRAS BARNECHEA, Raúl (1986). *Los cronistas del Perú y otros ensayos.* Lima: Banco de Crédito del Perú.

REGALADO DE HURTADO, Liliana (1984). En torno a la relación entre mitmaqkuna, poder y tecnología en los Andes. *Historia y Cultura* 17, Lima.

ROSTWOROWSKI DE DIEZ CANSECO, María (1983). *Estructuras andinas del poder.* Lima: Instituto de Estudios Peruanos.

ROSTWOROWSKI DE DIEZ CANSECO, María (1988). *Historia del Tawantinsuyo.* Lima: Instituto de Estudios Peruanos / CONCYTEC.

ROWE, John H. (1963). Inca Culture at the time of the Spanish Conquest. *Handbook of South American Indians,* II, second edition. New York: Cooper Square Publ.

WACHTEL, Nathan (1971). *La vision des Vaincus. Les Indiens du Pèrou devant la Conquete Espagnole, 1530-1570.* Paris: Galllimard.

ZUIDEMA, R. Tom (1964). *The Ceque System of Cuzco.* Leyden: Brill.

LIST OF CHRONICLES

ANÓNIMO (attributed to Cristobal de Mena) ([1534]1929). *La conquista del Perú, llamada la Nueva Castilla. Facsimile edition.* New York Public Library.

ANÓNIMO (attributed to Cristobal de Molina and Bartolomé de Segovia) ([1552-59]1943). Relación de muchas cosas acaecidas en el Perú en suma para entender a la letra la manera que se tuvo en la conquista y población de estos reinos...por manera que lo que aquí tratare más se podrá decir "Destrucción del Perú" que conquista ni población. In *Los pequeños grandes libros de Historia Americana.* Lima: Lib. e Imp. Miranda.

ANÓNIMO (attributed to Miguel de Estete) (1987). *Crónicas iniciales de la conquista del Perú.* Alberto Mario Salas (editor). Buenos Aires: Plus Ultra.

ARZANS DE ORSUA Y VELA, Bartolomé ([1735]1965). *Historia de la Villa Imperial de Potosí.* Providence: Brown University Press.

ÁVILA, Francisco ([¿1598?]1966). *Dioses y hombres de Huarichiri.* José María Arguedas (translator). Lima: Museo Nacional de Historia e Instituto de Estudios Peruanos.

BERTONIO, Ludovico ([1612]1956). *Vocabulario de la lengua aymara.* Facsimile edition. La Paz.

BETANZOS, Juan Diez de ([1551]1987). *Suma y narración de los Incas.* Madrid: Atlas.

CABELLO DE BALBOA, Miguel ([1586]1951). *Miscelánea Antártica.* Lima: Universidad de San Marcos.

CASAS, Bartolomé de las (1939). *De las antiguas gentes del Perú.* Colección de Libros y Documentos referentes a la historia del Perú. Tomo XI, Lima.

CASTRO, Cristóbal de & Diego ORTEGA MOREJÓN ([1558]1974). Relación del valle de Chincha. In Juan Carlos Crespo, La relación de Chincha (1558). *Historia y Cultura.* 8, Lima.

CIEZA DE LEÓN, Pedro de ([1553]1986). *Crónica del Perú. Primera Parte*. Lima: Fondo Editorial PUCP / Academia Nacional de la Historia.

CIEZA DE LEÓN, Pedro de ([1550]1985). *Crónica del Perú. Segunda Parte*. Lima: Fondo Editorial PUCP / Academia Nacional de la Historia.

COBO, Bernabé ([1653]1956). *Historia del Nuevo Mundo*. Francisco Mateos S.J. (ed.). Madrid: Biblioteca de Autores Españoles.

DIEZ DE SAN MIGUEL, Garci ([1567]1964). *Visita hecha a la provincia de Chucuito*. Lima: Casa de la Cultura del Perú.

GARCILASO DE LA VEGA, Inca ([1609]1943). *Comentarios reales de los Incas*. Angel Rosenblat (ed.). Buenos Aires: Emecé.

GOMARA, Francisco López de ([1552]1946). Historia de las Indias. In Enrique de Vedia, *Historiadores primitivos de Indias*. Madrid: Biblioteca de Autores Españoles.

GUAMÁN POMA DE AYALA, Felipe ([1615]1987). *Nueva Crónica y Buen Gobierno*. Franklin Pease (ed.). Caracas: Biblioteca Ayacucho.

GUTIÉRREZ DE SANTA CLARA, Pedro ([1603]1963). Quinquenarios o Historia de las guerras civiles del Perú. In Juan Pérez de Tudela (ed.), *Crónicas del Perú*. Madrid: Biblioteca de Autores Españoles.

JIMÉNEZ DE LA ESPADA, Marcos (ed.) (1879). *Tres relaciones de antigüedades peruanas*. Madrid: Ministerio de Fomento.

JIMÉNEZ DE LA ESPADA, Marcos (1965). *Relaciones Geográficas de Indias*. Second edition. Madrid: Biblioteca de Autores Españoles.

MORI, Juan de & Hernando Alonso MALPARTIDA ([1549]1967). La visitación de los pueblos de los indios. In Íñigo Ortiz de Zuñiga, *Visita de la provincia de León de Huánuco en 1562*. Huánuco: Universidad Nacional Hermilio Valdizán.

MURÚA, Martín de ([1616]1962-64). *Historia general del Perú. Origen y descendencia de los Incas*. Manuel Ballesteros Gaibrois (ed.). Madrid: Biblioteca de Autores Españoles.

OLIVA, Giovanni Anello ([¿1631?]1895). *Historia del reino y provincias del Perú.* Juan Pazos Varela & Luis Varela y Orbegozo (eds.). Lima: Impr. y Libr. de San Pedro.

ORTIZ DE ZÚÑIGA, Iñigo ([1562]1967-72). *Visita de la provincia de León de Huánuco en 1562.* John Murra (ed.). Huánuco: Universidad Nacional Hermilio Valdizán.

POLO DE ONDEGARDO, Juan (1916-1917). *Informaciones acerca de la religión y gobierno de los Incas.* Colección de Libros y Documentos referentes a la historia del Perú. Tomos III y IV, Lima.

SANTA CRUZ PACHACUTI YAMQUI SALCAMAYGUA, Joan de ([1613]1879). Relación de altiguedades deste reino del Pirú. In Marcos Jiménez de la Espada, *Tres relaciones de antigüedades peruanas.* Madrid: Ministerio de Fomento.

SANTILLÁN, Fernando de ([1563]1879). Relación. In Marcos Jiménez de la Espada, *Tres relaciones de antigüedades peruanas.* Madrid: Ministerio de Fomento.

SANTO TOMÁS, Domingo de ([1560]1951). *Lexicon o Vocabulario de la lengua general del Perú.* Facsimile Edition. Lima: Universidad de San Marcos.

SARMIENTO DE GAMBOA, Pedro ([1572]1947). *Segunda parte de la Historia General llamada Indica.* Ángel Rosenblat (ed.). Buenos Aires: EMECE.

TOLEDO, Francisco de ([1570]1940). Informaciones sobre los Incas. In Roberto Levillier, *Don Francisco de Toledo, Supremo Organizador del Perú. Su vida y su obra.* Tomo II. Buenos Aires: Espasa Calpe.

XEREZ, Francisco de ([1534]1987). Verdadera relación de la conquista del Perú. In Alberto Mario Salas (editor), *Crónicas iniciales de la conquista del Perú.* Buenos Aires: Plus Ultra.

ZÁRATE, Agustín de ([1555]1944). *Historia del descubrimiento y conquista del Perú.* Jan Kermenic (ed.). Lima: Libr. e Impr. Miranda.

Se terminó de imprimir en
los talleres gráficos de
Tarea Asociación Gráfica Educativa
Psje. María Auxiliadora 156, Breña
Correo e.: tareagrafica@terra.com.pe
Teléfono: 332-3229 Fax: 424-1582
Se utilizaron caracteres
Adobe Garamond Pro en 11.5 puntos
para el cuerpo del texto
Octubre 2015 Lima – Perú